A dream written down with a date becomes a goal. A goal broken down into steps becomes a plan. A plan backed by action makes your dreams come true.

—**Dr. Greg S. Reid**, entrepreneur, award-winning author, and film producer

SET YOUR OWN GOALS

Or Someone Else Will

How to Overcome Self-Limiting Beliefs and Get Things Done

Gary MacDermid

Foreword by
Rear Admiral Robert C. Nowakowski, U.S.Navy

Published by Cash Flow Press

Printed in the United States of America

Produced by GMK Writing and Editing, Inc.
Managing Editor: Katie Benoit
Copyedited by Amy Paradysz
Text design and composition by Libby Kingsbury
Proofread by Lissette Lorenz
Cover design by Libby Kingsbury
Printed by IngramSpark

Print ISBN: 979-8-9893952-7-9
Ebook EISN: 979-8-9893952-8-6

Note: *This publication is presented solely for informational, educational, and entertainment purposes. It is not intended to provide personal, business, financial, or other advice and should not be relied upon as such. If expert assistance is required, the services of a professional should be sought. The publisher and the author and their affiliated entities and individuals do not make any guarantees or other promises as to any results that may be obtained from using the content of this book. To the maximum extent permitted by law, the publisher and the author and their affiliated entities and individuals disclaim any and all liability in the unlikely event any information contained in this book inadvertently proves to be inaccurate, incomplete, or unreliable, or results any harm or loss. You, the reader, are responsible for your own choices, actions, and results.*

To my parents; and to my wife and children; and to those who have ever felt trapped living someone else's dream and the silent achievers who have always put others first

Acknowledgments

I'd like to thank Didi Wong for convincing me to appear on Amazon Prime Video's "Speak Up" series to share my platform for setting one's own goals and for convincing me to transform that appearance into this book. The book itself involved invaluable help from Gary M. Krebs and the team at GMK Writing and Editing, Inc.

The practices shared in the book were derived in large part from the wisdom of my mentor, John Burley. Many of the examples and anecdotes of the book come from my years of active duty in the United States Navy, and I want to thank the many shipmates and veterans I served with for imparting invaluable lessons to me about achievement, attention to detail, excellence, and character.

Finally, I'd like to thank Dr. Greg S. Reid and Roland Frasier for their example and inspiration.

Contents

Foreword

I met Lieutenant Commander MacDermid when he was assigned to my reserve unit in 2013. He worked directly under me as one of the four key personnel responsible for our unit's surface warfare capabilities as part of the United States Navy. We trained extensively for war games and frequently engaged in very intense situations. It was obvious that Lt. MacDermid was an extraordinary individual with a broad range of profound skills.

What struck me most about Lt. MacDermid was his intuition. He is clearly a rare individual who can see three, four, even five steps ahead. This is so valuable when planning, and I relied upon his insight on a regular basis. I was not surprised to learn that he was a chess champion as a child. Of course, it's also not surprising that he was a certified nuclear engineer as an adult, capable of understanding complex processes and overseeing massive operating systems with tremendous success.

Another remarkable quality of Lt. MacDermid—and one complimentary to his insight—was his communications skills. He spoke truth to power in a manner that was respectful yet candid. So often in situations that involve hierarchy—and the military is no exception—individuals simply don't tell the higher-ups what they need to hear. As a result, necessary information is not conveyed, and problems are not solved or avoided. This was never the case with Lt. MacDermid. He told me—and others—precisely what he thought or what he observed. There was no sugarcoating or misdirection. He told it like it was, and he did so in a manner that was clear, concise, and respectful.

Lt. MacDermid was my most trusted and valued aide. I had the ability as a commanding officer to fast-track one promotion, and there was no doubt about who this would be. He is a man of great character—an honest, reliable, hardworking individual—who was an incredible asset to our unit and to the U.S. Navy. Not surprisingly, he successfully transitioned into civilian life and has engineered a straightforward, clear, and insightful methodology for achieving personal goals. Of course, his desire to share his knowledge is what made Lt. MacDermid a great mentor in the Navy and a great contributor to society at large.

I found *Set Your Own Goals—or Someone Else Will* to be not just a "how-to" type of book for business success but also a blueprint for living a purposed life—one in which individuals have command of their own experiences and live a meaningful existence true to their own respective visions. This is a must read for anyone who desires a fresh, accessible guide to setting one's own goals and accomplishing them.

—Robert C. Nowakowski, Rear Admiral, U.S. Navy

Introduction

You might think that a man charged with operating the nuclear reactors of a U.S. Navy aircraft carrier—a floating city worth billions of dollars with a crew of thousands of military personnel—would be able to set his own goals. But I was unable to do it.

During my two decades of active and reserve service, I operated engineering, sonar, and weapons systems on ships. I led and trained hundreds of people on many complex nuclear, electrical, and operational warfare activities integral to the safety and security of our Navy's ships and our country's defense. And yet, when I went out on my own, I found myself unable to develop and sustain personal goals. It was almost as if I'd never considered doing anything for myself because I had been so blindly committed to achieving the mission. For most of my life, my priorities were: (1) my job; (2) my friends and family; and (3) my career.

I realized that my entire life up to that point had been following orders or agendas of other people. My bosses. My commanders. My vice presidents. My friends. My parents. I did every task they and others asked—or ordered—me to do, and I did them well. In every circumstance, I was able to apply myself to the assigned goal and get the job done at an extremely high level—whether it involved navigating a warship through the Persian Gulf in a combat zone or performing advanced testing and hazardous work for nuclear reactors. I was regarded as a "hard charger"—someone with an aggressive, get-the-job-done personality. I qualified first in most of the activities during nuclear training and was even selected amongst the top 5 percent of the Navy to receive an engineering scholarship and my commission as a Naval Officer through the new Seaman to Admiral 21st Century program.

I gained a great deal from my service and don't regret a single moment of it. However, there was one critical skill I wasn't taught: *How to recognize myself as an individual person enough to create significant goals and believe I could achieve them.* I soon found out that I wasn't alone in this situation; many people I encountered—not just veterans—had either never created goals of their own or lacked confidence that they would achieve anything extraordinary beyond what they were currently doing in the confines of their present jobs.

Don't get me wrong. I understand why much of the world works this way, especially when you're starting out and building your skills and resume. There is also something to be said for knowing your place in the food chain, following orders and a chain of command under certain circumstances. However, this mindset can often create self-limiting beliefs, especially when there is a perception that someone who is born into a certain wealth or education level is destined to remain there.

If you are an entrepreneur or a small business owner—or

are working in a corporate environment and hoping to venture down one of these paths at some point in your life—you may not even realize that you have been held back because you followed goals or adopted a mindset that was influenced—if not dictated—by other people. Now it's your turn to take control of your present and future by releasing those constraints, ditching any self-limiting beliefs, creating meaningful and impactful goals, and fulfilling your innermost wishes and dreams.

By following my methodology, you will regain control of your ambitions and get things done in a productive way you never imagined, even if you are (or have been) exposed to negative-thinking people. You'll experience a complete mindset shift that will enable you to believe in yourself, visualize your path, and most importantly, make it happen.

How This Book Is Organized

By intent, I didn't want this book to be like your father's business book or a self-help guide. I'm introducing this as a new approach to both these genres, hopefully making it as contemporary, accessible, and actionable as possible.

I've divided the content into three parts:

- **Part One: Laying the Groundwork**

  ◊ *Chapter One, "Taking the Self-Assessment"*:
    We begin with a self-assessment that helps you determine how much control you've had over your life and career to this point—and how well it's worked for you.

◊ **Chapter Two, "Understanding the Language of Goal Setting":** I explain the often-confusing terminology surrounding goals.

◊ **Chapter Three, "Getting S.M.A.R.T.":** I break down the S.M.A.R.T. acronym and demonstrate why it's so important.

• **Part Two: Establishing the Right Mindset**

◊ **Chapter Four, "Shifting Your Thoughts":** We explore how to adopt changes in thinking that allow for the actualization of your goals.

◊ **Chapter Five, "Making the Three Essential Mindset Shifts":** We explore the three crucial mindset shifts you make to accomplish your goals: *believe it before you see it; abundance over scarcity;* and *positioning yourself for success.*

• **Part Three: Taking the Five Steps to Achieving Your Goals**

◊ **Chapter Six, "Step One—Visualizing the Process":** Visualization works, as proven by the significant number of accomplished people who regularly practice this technique.

◊ **Chapter Seven, "Step Two—Seeking Counsel":** If

you want to achieve the best results, you must consult with the best.

◊ *Chapter Eight, "Step Three—Working Backwards, Setting Targets":* Start from the end—what you would like to accomplish—and then backtrack to identify the specific actions you must take to get there.

◊ *Chapter Nine, "Step Four—Writing It Down and Saying It Aloud":* Unless you memorialize your goals in writing and refer to them often, they will become like air and float away.

◊ *Chapter Ten, "Step Five—Finding a Suitable Accountability Partner":* An accountability partner isn't your expert counsel but rather someone who is in the trenches with you and helping you stay on track.

◊ *Chapter Eleven, "A Special Bonus—Zones":* We'll keep you in suspense on the bonus until you get there!

Along the way, I provide boxed tips, referred to as "Goal Tending," and anecdotes from my experiences and those of others. We'll pause every now and then to arm you with what you need to fight against threats that challenge, block, or even threaten your goals.

Let's get started—full speed ahead!

PART ONE

Laying
the
Groundwork

1

Taking the Self-Assessment

"Knowing yourself is the beginning of all wisdom."—ARISTOTLE

When we are children, we are beholden to the decisions of our parents—which is a good thing, since they support us, raise us, and keep us safe. As we hit adolescence, we begin to think independently and develop a sense of self-determination and outcome. We dream big, think big, and are often fearless. Perhaps we even rebel a bit against the authority figures in our lives. We think we know everything—or at least more than our parents—and assert ourselves in both appropriate and inappropriate ways. Hopefully, we learn, grow, and mature, and start making wise, responsible decisions on our own, albeit with support and counsel from parents, close relatives, friends, teachers, supervisors, colleagues, and coaches.

Do the core decisions you made throughout the early part of your life's journey feed into fulfilling your biggest hopes and dreams? Since you're reading this book, I think it's safe to say *probably not.*

It's possible you received higher education of some sort. If so, were you able to attend and graduate from your university of choice—or did you settle for something less or different because of financial constraints or due to family pressure? Did you select a major that you were passionate about?

The next stages involve making career decisions, choosing a place to live, and pursuing relationships. In the beginning, it seems like the world is your oyster and you have free will to do whatever your heart desires—but is this really the case?

The fact of the matter is that most people live according to the expectations of other people and the circumstances at the time. For example, your parents may have expectations that you become a doctor, lawyer, or engineer, so you follow that path due to familial pressure or to please certain family members. Next thing you know, you have an expensive degree, a lifetime of college loans to pay back, and a career that has been prescribed for you but may not be fulfilling.

The same type of situation occurs when your parents expect you to enter the family business or a trade that has been a family legacy. Your grandfather and father were butchers, so naturally you became one, too. Many careers—military, teaching, auto mechanic, and nursing, to name a few—circulate within the family construct and become generational. For individuals raised in these environments, other options may not even be mentioned as a possibility.

In my case, I never remotely thought about or wanted a career in the military, but my father decided this for me because of our economic situation. The only choice I had was which military branch I was going to enter. Little did I know at the time that this was going to be my life for the next two decades.

What sacrifices did you make years ago that have led to your present situation? Perhaps you were unaware at the time that decisions made for you in the beginning were digging you deeper into a hole from which you couldn't burrow out.

Take the questionnaire below to find out if following other people's goals have caused you to form limiting beliefs that have stifled your ambitions and dreams.

The Self-Assessment

In your journal, in a notebook, or on a blank sheet of paper, rate each question below as honestly as you can on a scale of 1–10, with ten being the highest.

1. You are currently in the industry or line of work that you want to be in: _____

2. You are currently earning your desired income: _____

3. You have determined your career path with little influence from your parents or other close family members. You may have been inspired by them or their careers, but you chose your path because of your own belief and desires: _____

4. Friends, family, and others in your circle are currently positive, encouraging, and supportive of your efforts to enter your desired career path: _____

5. You have always been able to tune out negativity from others about your career path: _____

6. You have always maintained faith that someday you would achieve your career ambitions and financial
   success: _____

7. Your setbacks toward achieving your career ambitions have always been within your control to achieve. _____

8. You have already achieved milestones that you believe will lead you to fulfilling your career ambitions. _____

9. You have identified any gaps in your personal development or mindset that have held you back from achieving your desired career ambitions. _____

10. You have a mentor at the level you want to reach who is helping guide you on achieving your career ambitions. _____

Now add up your numbers to determine your score:

90–100: You are a champion goal achiever!
80–90: You are on your way and just need a boost to get on track.

70–80: You've been "getting by," but other people, obstacles, and disappointments have held you back.
Under 70: Other people have created goals for you, and you feel your career ambitions have dimmed.

In the sections and chapters that follow, I will guide you through my process to help you overcome self-limiting beliefs, get things done, become a champion goal achiever, and fulfill your dreams and destiny. You are probably wondering why I am so confident that it is possible for anyone at any stage to accomplish this. The answer is simple: At one time, my self-assessment score was at rock bottom—a situation I believe is all too common.

Let's start with a simplified version of the questionnaire with how I would have answered them years ago when I began my professional career, to illustrate where I stood:

1. *Question:* Do you like what you're doing?
   Answer: No. (0 out of 10)

2. *Question:* Why are you doing what you do?
   Answer: I don't know. (0 out of 10)

3. *Question:* Why did you choose that job?
   Answer: I didn't. (0 out of 10)

4. *Question:* Was it related to something you wanted to do?
   Answer: No. (0 out of 10)

5. *Question:* Was it because of something somebody else thought that you should do?
   Answer: Yes. (0 out of 10)

Note the irony: My total score would have been *zero*. As I wrote in the Introduction, my goals were handed to me by other people. I don't think you need to have served in the military to be able to relate to my story.

Within a month from when I left the Navy, headhunters set me up on about five interviews based on my experience and skills. The effort led to four solid job opportunities that paid roughly the same. The positions were in various locations around the country. I accepted one of them—an engineering consultant role for a company that served the nuclear power industry.

Was this my dream job? No. Was it even something I wanted to do? Again, no. I took the job because it was conveniently found for me, it paid a certain amount of money, and I had family members living nearby.

This is a pattern for a lot of people who enter the professional ranks. One poll reported that only 20 percent of people set their own goals and, among that group, 70 percent fail to achieve them. It's no wonder that, according to a recent Gallup survey, 85 percent of people hate their jobs. (They also dislike their bosses, but that's an issue for a separate book.)

Trust me: There is a much better way for you to discover and follow your path, and I will help you get there. First, we must distinguish important terms that are often confused or misunderstood; I'm talking about *vision, mission, purpose, values*, *strategy*, and *goals*. All these things play key roles for you personally and in your career—whether you are an entrepreneur, own a business, are employed by a small business or corporate enterprise, or serve in a nonprofit setting.

2

Understanding the Language
of Goal Setting

"All that we are is the result of what we have thought."
—Buddha

Before we address the main topic of this book—*goals*—we need to identify all the terminology you must know before officially starting the goal-setting process. There are many ways to tackle this subject. My preferred approach is to break the concepts down in order of how they should be created if you are just starting out as an entrepreneur or business owner—although, of course, the information applies to anyone in the corporate world or just seeking to hit the next career milestone. I break it down like this: vision, mission, purpose, values, strategy, and then ... wait for it ... *goals*!

Vision

A vision may be created for an individual, a team, a product (or line of products), or an entire business. In either case, a vision—known formally as a *vision statement*—describes in a few words *what* the desired state of the entity will look like five or ten years down the road—aka, in the future. In a company setting, a vision statement provides a clear picture for everyone to understand where the company is headed.

By intent, a vision statement is aspirational and grandiose and not necessarily literal or measurable. For example, LinkedIn's vision is as follows: "To create economic opportunity for every member of the global workforce." Is it truly possible for LinkedIn to give every single person in the world an economic boost? Of course not—but that is what their utopia looks like, and they strive to get as close as possible to making it come to fruition.

Your vision becomes your guiding principle, your North Star. If you have a documented personal vision, you will never feel lost, as everything is a step along your journey, and you can always recalibrate if you happen to get off track. Similarly, if you are a company leader and hold everyone in your organization accountable to your vision, the team will remain focused and unified.

Mission

A *mission statement*, distinct from a vision statement, identifies *how* the business is going to turn the vision into reality. The best mission statements offer an emotional promise of how they intend to improve the lives of others with specific examples. Let's look at Apple's mission statement as a prime example: "To bring the best user experience to customers through innovative hardware, software, and services." In just a few words, Apple has stated how people will be impacted ("the best user experience") and how they will do it ("through innovative hardware, software, and services").

Goal Tending

In the military, a mission refers to a specific task or operation that must be completed by one or more persons within a designated area and time frame. Often, "going on a mission" implies some form of battle occurring in another country. During my service with the Navy, we planned many high-level, important missions, although the majority were for practice. Despite being in many "hot zones"—meaning, locations rife with potential imminent danger—I can be thankful I never experienced physical combat.

The thing everyone in the military understands is that practice is essential to the military's protocol for preparedness. There is no room for error when it comes to military exercises. Tasks are repeated until everyone gets it 100 percent right. One of the things we learn in the military is that, when things get tough (aka "the s**t hits the fan"), we default to our level of our training (or preparedness). Practice helps us develop muscle memory, so we will be able to perform well in the heat of battle. It's not a far cry from the "wax on, wax off" lesson Mr. Miyagi teaches Daniel in the first *Karate Kid* film, in which the sensei orders his young pupil to wax his cars with certain motions using each hand one at a time.

When I was aboard a naval ship, I learned how to practice exiting while blindfolded, in case of an emergency, such as a fire, and you can't see through the smoke. In your life, think about how you can incorporate practice into your daily activities to perfect what you do and be prepared for any potential worst-case scenario.

A personal mission statement can prove valuable to you, as it will show you how you are going to attain your personal vision and make it easier for you to achieve. Sometimes a personal mission statement can help sharpen the focus of your resume and enable you to stand out from other candidates if you are on a job search. If, for example, you are seeking a sales position, you might write something like this (the *how* part is italicized): "To electrify sales based on *my thirty years of proven results and substantial network of trusted industry relationships.*"

Purpose

If vision is the *what* and mission is the *how,* where does *purpose* fit in? If you guessed that it represents your *why,* you would be correct. Purpose is your company's reason for being and the meaning or significance behind what you do. If you think it's just about "making money," you need to probe much deeper. A well-defined purpose identifies *the impact* you have on others and implies what makes you unique. Dick's Sporting Goods, for example, may not be saving the world, but it has a powerful purpose that is distinct in the marketplace: "We create confidence and excitement by personally equipping all athletes to achieve their dreams."

An integral part of purpose is *passion* (and not in the romantic sense). A powerful purpose fuels your desire to continue striving to achieve your vision, no matter what. Without such passion, you would give up at the first obstacle and not have enough ambition and fortitude to complete essential goals that build your ideal future.

Values

Many individuals and businesses also create a set of *values* that internally and externally represent the company. I am not necessarily referring to religious values, although that might be the case for evangelical organizations or those that seek to foster a spiritual culture. Most often, values are comprised of the following three things:

1. *Principles*—such as acting with integrity, taking responsibility.

2. *Beliefs and attitudes*—such as respect, equality, reliability, dedication to quality.

3. *Standards of behavior*—such as professionalism, safe practices.

Many organizations create a separate list of principles, define codes of behavior in an employee manual, or hold leader and employee training sessions to reduce the risk of gray area in determining what is acceptable behavior as decisions are being made (and, therefore, reducing chance of lawsuits). If you are an entrepreneur or sole proprietor, it's a good idea to make a list of values as reminders for yourself, as you may not have people around you to nudge you as things go off-course or point out your blind spots.

In today's business climate, younger generations—Millennials (born 1981–1996), Gen Z (born 1997–2012), and Alpha (born 2013–2025)—are especially keen on working for companies that care about employees and society, which means values matter for recruitment and retention. Many people born since 1981 won't conduct business with or buy products from a company that doesn't treat employees fairly, produce products that are safe for people and the environment, or demonstrate ethical practices. People look for businesses to be authentic and transparent with their values and hold true to them; those that breach such trust (such as a factory that dumps toxic liquid into drinking water) pay a severe price in terms of brand loyalty.

Strategy

Now we get to the nuts and bolts, as it were. *Strategy* is the methodology, process, or plan you put in place to pursue and achieve your goals. You want to think of yourself as an archer about to launch an arrow; strategy is your target.

A concrete strategy is essential in any business scenario—entrepreneurship, small business ownership, a franchise, a private company of any size, or a corporate entity—as it outlines precisely what actions you will and will not take. Without an effective strategy in place, the chances of accomplishing your goals become greatly diminished. An organization is likely to create myriad strategies, all of which feed into the vision, mission, purpose, and values. There can be an overarching corporate strategy, but then separate strategies for each department: sales, marketing, production, and so on.

Over the years, you've probably heard a great deal about "military strategy" in terms of the United States defense efforts, which obviously includes the Navy. The overarching Naval strategy is to "defend the Homeland with an assured nuclear deterrent from beneath the sea to deter nuclear and non-nuclear strategic attacks." While specific military strategies are classified (and business strategies are usually kept confidential) a fact sheet lays out three priorities: "integrated deterrence, or coordinating military, diplomatic and economic levers from across the U.S. government to deter an adversary from taking an aggressive action; 'campaigning forward' to build up the capability of international coalitions and complicate adversaries' actions; and building enduring advantages through investing in the right technologies and people."

Whether you are in the military or in business, the objective of any strategy is to gain a specific competitive advantage. Strategies might involve growth, expansion, or diversification. A business strategy might be like "Build out our online B to C retail business and increase our industry market share by 15 percent in the next year." Note that the strategy doesn't get into the nitty-gritty of how the strategy will be accomplished, as it might entail several steps involving many different departments and people. This is where our central theme comes into play...

Goals

Now for the billion-dollar question: What is a *goal?* In simple terms, a goal is an objective or something that you're trying to achieve based on your defined strategy. Goals may fall into one of three categories, which often overlap—especially if you own your own business:

1. *Personal:* These are goals that offer a perceived benefit to our physical, mental, and/or emotional health. Such goals might involve creating or deepening relationships (with partners, friends, or relatives); physical conditioning (such as training to bench press a certain amount of weight); hobbies (such as completing work on building a treehouse for the kids); educational pursuits (such as learning a foreign language); or widening your horizons (such as traveling across Europe). These goals can be as strict or casual as you want them to be.

2. *Professional:* This type of goal fits into two potential camps. The first is what might be desirable in terms of advancing your career, such as completing tasks you think will lead to earning a promotion or changing jobs and getting a better title in another organization. A professional goal might also refer to changing your career trajectory if you are looking to tackle a new challenge or are unhappy with your current functions. The second bucket of professional goals includes assignments, tasks, and projects—individual or team-related—that are specifically designed

to benefit your organization. In many cases, organizations provide top-down goals that cascade from the chief executive officer (who sometimes has directives from the board or investors), to executives, to department heads (directors), to teams, to individuals. The benefit of this process is that company goals function better when there is transparency and synergy from top to bottom and sideways within an organization and everyone is rowing in the same direction to achieve mutually beneficial results. The downside of this process is that the goals can sometimes end up assigned to workers without their collaborative input. Of course, we will be discussing all aspects of professional goals in much greater detail throughout the book and what you can do to maximize the benefits of the process.

3. *Financial:* As the cliché goes, "Money makes the world go round." Financial goals, which may be short- or long-term, could include saving up a certain amount of money to buy a house or car or paying down college loans by a certain date. Companies often have annual revenue targets, which are usually broken down further by quarter and month. If your position involves producing revenue—such as in business development or sales—financial goals can override other goals and cause a great deal of stress.

As you continue your journey in this book, reflect in a journal or notebook on which of the above three categories your goals have fallen into—personal, professional, or financial—and answer the following questions:

- Was there some overlap among the three, especially between personal and professional?

- Did your personal, professional, and financial goals ever clash with each other?

- Were your professional goals handed down to you by a supervisor or did you work on them collaboratively?

- How many of your goals were successfully completed?

- How many of your goals are you currently on track to complete?

- Which category did most of your successful goals fit into?

- Which categories did most of your unsuccessful goals fit into?

The Importance of Goals

Why do we need goals? They provide motivation and reminders, but they are far more important than that. Goals provide *control* over your life. As the subtitle of this book states, if you don't set your own goals, someone else will do this for you. This means another person is directing what you do with your time—and there is nothing more valuable than our time on this earth and how we choose to spend it. When we put ourselves in this situation, we lose agency over our own lives and stop growing. We either plateau or shrink. As Nigerian-born British poet Ben Okri once wrote, "Our time here is magic! It's the only space you have to realize whatever it is that is beautiful, whatever is true, whatever is great, whatever is potential, whatever is rare, whatever is unique…"

Setting our own goals provides tangible action steps we can take to improve the lives of ourselves and others. Unlike the other terms explored in this chapter—vision, mission, purpose, value, and strategy—goals aren't soft, squishy, or subject to interpretation. When properly drafted, they move the needle forward on all the other terminology, bringing you a step closer to your vision. You can check a completed goal off your To Do list or whiteboard and then celebrate a win. You can toast yourself or treat yourself to something special. Why not? You deserve it. Not only does this feel great, it also gives you that extra lift to demonstrate that you can accomplish whatever you set your mind to doing. It makes pushing forward on your subsequent goal all that much easier.

Now that you understand all the jargon, it's time for you to get S.MA.R.T.—with your goals, that is.

3

Getting S.M.A.R.T.

"A goal properly set is halfway reached."—Zig Ziglar

In many organizations—especially large corporate ones—goals are generated at the executive level and then filter down to the director level, to each department, and then to every team member. These are known as top-down goals. The idea is that the goals become inextricably connected with each employee contributing to the most important areas laid out by the company's CEO and/or leadership team. Often the Human Resources (HR) department will play a significant role facilitating this process, ensuring that the puzzle pieces fit together as much as possible.

Sometimes top-down goals will work for you, and sometimes they don't. In an ideal scenario, when it's goal-setting time in an organization, the middle managers will present the executive goals and their goals to the team and work with members to create five to seven smaller team goals that align with executive goals while also accounting for individual strengths and developmental or improvement needs. Unfortunately, this isn't what typically occurs. Often, the middle managers simply pass executive goals down to the workforce with minimal changes or input from the workforce themselves.

In these situations, workers have little to no say about their annual goals, which makes tremendous sense from a purely one-sided organizational standpoint. A certain amount of alignment is important or else the company becomes topsy-turvy with everyone heading in different directions. We might not like how this is handled—at least until we look at it from the opposite perspective: "Bottom-up" goals don't exactly make sense, right?

The ideal scenario is for the middle manager to share the executive and department goals and then invite the team to draft their own goals based on the cascading list. Once those goals have been drafted, the middle manager has an opportunity to sit down with each employee and provide feedback. This meeting of the minds ensures alignment while also affording workers at every level the opportunity to play an active role in the process.

Sometimes employees are granted the benefit of a "development goal": learning a skill that helps a person perform their responsibilities better or at a more sophisticated level. Occasionally, there are also "stretch goals" offered, if the tasks involved are more challenging than the individual's regular job functions and/or the individual seeks; to gain knowledge that might lead to career advancement (such as leadership roles) or just a different trajectory (such moving to a different department); and financial basics or retirement planning.

Over the years, the process of goal setting has evolved to ensure the greatest chance of success while employing a consistent methodology. The main objectives are as follows:

- Be sure the goals are recorded in writing and reviewed at the end of each calendar year (if not also every month and each quarter to determine progress).

- Find a comfort zone for all parties involved that facilitates company and individual growth.

- Strive to reach a high standard.

- Align goals with the company vision and purpose.

- Provide enhanced training or cross-training for employees as needed to align with the company's vision and purpose.

- Meet the company's growth and revenue needs.

- Create an action plan that establishes an even playing field among all employees while playing to their strengths.

- Complete action plan assignments on time.

- Establish key performance indicators (KPIs) to ensure that progress is properly tracked through an efficient and consistent methodology.

Implementing all the above and getting everything right seems like a truly daunting task, don't you think? Thankfully, in 1981, a consultant named George Doran (along with Arthur Miller and James Cunningham) published a paper entitled "There's a S.M.A.R.T. Way to Write Management's Goals and Objectives," which detailed a foolproof goal-setting process. By playing on the word "smart" to create the memorable acronym, Doran laid out a practical, easy-to-follow foundation that has since become common practice for organizations of all sizes. Whether you work for another company, own a business, or are seeking to go out on your own, I encourage you to create your own personal and career S.M.A.R.T. goals using the formula outlined in the pages that follow and adhering to the guidance throughout this book.

S.M.A.R.T. Is an Art

S.M.A.R.T. goals—which we used in the Navy—are a simple and effective way to itemize exactly what you want to achieve with an end date that brings closure to the effort, enabling you to subsequently move on to other things. If they are written properly, they can serve as daily reminders of what you need to accomplish. As mentioned, they need to fit with your vision and purpose, which means they require a certain amount of passion, so you are inherently driven to stick to them.

Some people consider S.M.A.R.T. goals to be short-term only. Personally, I don't view this as a negative. When handled properly, S.M.A.R.T goals serve as vital building blocks that contribute to the larger vision. Once a set of goals has been checked off, it becomes an easy matter to create new ones that will take you and/or the enterprise one step closer to achieving your idyllic future.

This is how the acronym breaks down:

S = Specific: the targeted area of what needs to get done; it must be written in such a way that anyone can read it and clearly understand what must be accomplished.

M = Measurable: the goal must be quantifiable in some way; it could be in terms of the number of new clients brought in, revenue earned, or a percentage increase in performance.

A = Achievable: sometimes the "A" represents "attainable," but the meaning is the same. The goal may be challenging, but it must be something that may be realistically accomplished. If the goal is insurmountable, it will mean wasted time and effort and everyone will become frustrated.

R = Relevant: the goal needs to be important and fit with the overall vision and purpose of the organization; if it doesn't, the initiative might just be more of a distraction than a priority.

T = Time Bound: the completion date. It is crucial for this to be specific; if it isn't, the goal can stretch out forever and will never get done.

Now let's see a S.M.A.R.T. goal in action using a simple, relatable example: weight loss. While creating the goal isn't foolproof—there is never a "guarantee"—following the S.M.A.R.T. paradigm does dramatically increase the chance of success because it holds the individual accountable.

Here's an example of a "not so smart goal": *I want to be thin.*

The individual who writes the above goal as stated is likely to fail because it is vague and not worded in a way that is *specific, measurable, achievable,* or *time bound.* While it may be desirable *to be thin* and therefore fits the *relevant* criteria, that alone isn't enough to see the goal all the way through to fruition.

Let's look at the same goal, but we'll smarten it up a bit:

I am going to work out at the gym five days a week and lose fifteen pounds, making me thinner by December 31 of this year.

Here's why the above statement is S.M.A.R.T.:

S = **Specific:** *going to the gym five days a week* is specific.

M = **Measurable:** *losing fifteen pounds* is measurable by standing on a scale.

A = **Achievable:** *losing fifteen pounds* is realistic and attainable for this person.

R = **Relevant:** the individual will look better, feel better, and be physically healthier by *being thinner,* so this certainly qualifies as important and is most likely aligned with personal goals.

T = **Time Bound:** *by December 31* offers an end date for the individual to work toward losing the weight daily.

Goal Tending

While you want your S.M.A.R.T. goal to be time bound with a final date, it can also be beneficial to create mini *milestones* that must be accomplished along the way at various checkpoints. This is akin to accountability and will help ensure you are on track. Sometimes having 25 percent and 50 percent milestone completion dates forces you to pay attention to your pace and progress. If, for example, you were supposed to have 25 percent of the goal completed by April 1 but only have 15 percent done, you'll have received a wakeup call to spur you into going faster or into trying a different approach to get back on schedule.

When I was a consultant for nuclear power plants, we had milestones during our design process at 25 percent of completion and then again at 50 percent. Each time, we would conduct a full review with the customer. If we were behind, we'd come up with a recovery plan to compensate for the delay. There was no other option. Imagine if we had waited until a month before the 100 percent deadline to take a hard look at our progress; we wouldn't have had the ability to make up for the lost time.

Milestone check-ins can sometimes be a bit scary, but it's much better to find out if you are behind sooner rather than later. If a customer is involved, awareness and transparency about your progress are always the best policies.

Once a S.M.A.R.T. goal has been firmly established, it provides the essential structure to help you see it through to fruition. The only remaining ingredient? *Discipline.* At this stage, the *how* needs to be applied. This breaks the goal down into manageable pieces with even more specifics assigned to it. For example, you might create a calendar of days and times you will go to the gym. It can be taken a step further by creating an exercise schedule itemizing what activities will be done at the gym and when:

- *Mondays and Wednesdays at 3:00 p.m.:* run on the treadmill for 30 minutes

- *Tuesdays and Thursdays at 4:00 p.m.:* lift weights for one hour

- *Saturdays 8:00 a.m.:* join a one-hour cardio class

We will cover the five steps to achieving your goals in greater detail in Part Three.

Act S.M.A.R.T.

Are you tracking with me so far? I hope so, because it's time for us to get real and apply the S.M.A.R.T. process to one of your goals. One of the best ways to accomplish this is to create a broad desirable goal and then break it down into S.M.A.R.T. components.

BROAD GOAL:

I am going to increase profitability of my company this year.

S.M.A.R.T. GOAL:

I am going to bring in five new clients and increase my company's profits 10 percent by the end of next quarter (December 31).

The S.M.A.R.T. breakdown:

S = Specific: *I will bring in five new clients by December 31.*

M = Measurable: *Each new client will be worth a minimum of $100K in revenue each year ($500K+ total).*

A = Achievable: *Last quarter, I brought in four new clients, so I think I can do one more in the coming quarter.*

R = Relevant: *My costs are going up 5%, so I need to increase my client base to offset the increase.*

T = Time Bound: *December 31 is the end of my quarter year, so it's the perfect time to assess whether I've brought in the requisite number of clients and increased my profit.*

Now it's your turn! On a separate sheet of paper or in a notebook, write out the S.M.A.R.T. template and fill in the blanks with one of your goals. Make sure that the goal you choose fits in with your vision and purpose and you have enough passion to sustain the goal.

Broad Goal:

_____

The S.M.A.R.T. breakdown:

S = Specific:

_____

M = Measurable:

_____

A = Achievable:

_____

R = Relevant:

_____

T = Time Bound:

_____

Milestones (deliverables and dates):

25 percent:

_____

50 percent:

_____

75 percent:

_____

Congratulations—we've laid down all the groundwork! We are ready to head to Part Two, where we'll tackle everything that you need to know to get into the right mindset for initiating and successfully completing your goals.

PART TWO

Establishing
the
Right
Mindset

4

Shifting Your Thoughts

"Change your thoughts and you change your world."
—NORMAN VINCENT PEALE

My career journey was not linear. I didn't find my destined path right away; it took two decades for me to get on the right track. Like most people, I paid my dues, so to speak, and had my share of challenges, detours, and derailments.

In my first job, I grinded it out as busboy in a diner. I took on increasing responsibility, becoming the assistant manager before I graduated from high school at seventeen. I enlisted in the Navy because I didn't have sufficient funds to pay for college. I was accepted amongst the top 5 percent of the Navy for a commissioning program to be a Naval Officer. I earned my degree in electrical engineering in three years, even though my freshman advisor told me it was impossible to do so in three years. After my naval career, I earned my Professional Engineer (PE) license and did several design and analysis projects for nuclear power plants around the country.

After having worked so hard to gain the right education and experience that brought me to that point, how was I able to transition into becoming a business owner, private equity investor, and public speaker? It was all due to one thing: *making the right mindset shifts that sustained my goal-setting process.*

Part of me wishes I'd had all this knowledge when I started out over two decades ago—it would have saved me a lot of time, money, energy, and frustration. On the other hand, my career evolution has enabled me to fully grasp the importance of mindset and develop my winning formula, which I will now share with you.

Insecurity, Self-Doubt, and Fear

Insecurity, self-doubt, and fear—these three toxic words can be powerful adversaries. Sometimes fear is launched at you from external forces, creating or increasing your level of insecurity and self-doubt. Other times, these feelings come from within; it may be biological or stem from deep psychological trauma triggered by stressful events. I empathize with you if you've been cursed with the double-whammy of external doubt and internal fear, as one feeds off the other and holds you back in ways both seen and unseen.

A good portion of negative thinking has the effect of brainwashing on the human mind. While some critical thinking can often be beneficial to distinguish fact from fiction, unsubstantiated, irrational negative energy will derail you from accomplishing even the simplest of goals. The human brain can be a complex and tricky organ, influencing you toward either success or failure. If your mind is convinced that failure is inevitable, it will involuntarily do everything it can to ensure this outcome, including induce you into a state of laziness. It's as if your mind is telling you, "Why bother? You're going to screw it up anyway." Later you'll hear the voice inside your head saying, "See? I told you so!"

The good news is that, like any kind of brainwashing, insecurity, self-doubt, and negative thought can be reversed and even undone. You simply require the right tools.

Strategically Share Your Goals to Avoid Common Setbacks

As stated in previous chapters, well-crafted S.M.A.R.T. goals move you forward along your path toward achieving your vision. This journey is driven by passion, which sometimes involves heavy emotions. This is generally a good thing, as passion fuels determination. The problem surfaces when you become so enthusiastic about your plans that you can't contain yourself. You have an irresistible urge to get on a megaphone—or post a message on a large social network—and trumpet your objectives to everyone.

Unfortunately, friends, family, and past/present colleagues who hear your plans don't always share your sense of optimism about your chances of success. Many of them believe they're helping you by adding logic, reason, and a dose of perceived reality to your efforts, whether you ask for these things or not. Many of them provide advice because they sincerely don't want to see you hurt, suffer failure, or waste your time or money. They may not know or understand your area of interest at all, but suddenly come across as authorities. "You want to write and publish a novel? That's really hard, isn't it? Are you sure anyone would be interested?" Then there are others who may have hidden agendas—such as envy—and may rain on your parade because they were either unsuccessful chasing their dreams or lacked the courage to even try.

I think you'll be able to relate to my story. After my military service and transition to civilian life, I became employed as an engineer in corporate America. After many years as an engineer, I realized that it wasn't what I wanted to do with my life. I gave the matter a great deal of thought, creating a vision with a set of supportive goals to get me started. Filled with excitement, I shared my plans with anyone and everyone in my circle who would listen. Some people—mostly the higher-ups and a few entrepreneurs I'd encountered outside of work—were supportive and encouraging. Entrepreneurs, who have "been there and done that," tend to understand the guts and fortitude required to venture out on your own with just an idea. It's rare you'll ever hear an independent entrepreneur say, "Hmm, I don't think it'll work." In fact, often they'll run with the attitude of "How can I *make* it work?"

Unfortunately, other well-meaning people—my parents, coworkers, and a few friends—were doubters who expressed concerns that it was unwise to exit a secure stable corporate job with benefits and a guaranteed salary to enter uncharted territory, especially during the COVID-19 pandemic. Ironically, some of them were the same people who had often spouted the cliché, "You can achieve anything you set out to do."

"Hey, I want to start my own business," I would breathlessly say. "I'm thinking real estate or private equity."

The responses would fire at me like nuclear missiles:

Are you kidding me?

In this economy? Are you crazy?

Why would you give up such a good, stable job?

Isn't it too late? Aren't other people your age far ahead of you?

Did you know that most startups fail?

What about job security? You have a wife, kids, and a mortgage.

It's not as easy as you think. You will just end up back here, anyway.

I didn't understand their objections. It wasn't as if I'd announced that I was flying to the moon or quitting my job to try out for the National Basketball Association. I simply wanted to start my own business, become financially independent, and do what I wanted with my life—which included spending more time with my friends and family. Why was it so hard to believe that I could pivot and accomplish something else? Why didn't it occur to them that, if I were to listen to their advice and push the idea aside, I'd never have a chance to find out if I even had the capability of succeeding?

To the doubters, it probably sounded as if I was planning to raise unicorns on a farm. They may have had their hearts in the right place, but they just didn't get it. People are programmed to view you only one way, especially if you've spent a long time in the same profession and seem to be good at it.

Their reactions gave me self-doubt that I hadn't experienced before. My parents and the other skeptics had planted weeds in my blooming garden. "What if they are right?" I asked myself.

I was able to kill off this external doubt but, for many people, the former often overtakes positivity. For this reason, the best bet is to be cautious with whom you share your goals and dreams, as resistance from others is to be expected. You can count on it happening right away when you are the height of your excitement, which is why I recommend keeping your goals and dreams to yourself.

Unfortunately, there are times when your plans might leak out to well-intended but negative-sounding people. If this occurs, be strong! Accept the fact that there will *always* be naysayers who don't understand what you are trying to accomplish. They may be smart people but not know about your field, your goals, or your abilities. Just because you haven't done something yet doesn't in any way imply you can't or won't be able to succeed.

I will never forget when a former colleague said to me, "You'll be back." Instead of allowing my mind to question what I was doing and allow his negative energy to corrupt my thoughts, I took his statement as a challenge. When you face a naysayer, there is nothing more gratifying than being able to prove them wrong.

If you have a need to broadcast yet can't find someone you believe will be completely supportive, I suggest you recruit a trusted coach or mentor. You want to actively search for a professional who knows how and when to listen versus others who dispense unsolicited advice that might bring you down, if not cause you to hold you back and second-guess. (We'll cover seeking counsel in greater detail in Chapter Seven.)

Mindset Matters

Let's talk about mindset. The importance of this cannot be

overemphasized, as it directs how we approach every idea and decision and, therefore, our outcomes.

Mindset is more than just the thoughts that happen to be rolling around in your head. It's about your *attitudes* toward your thoughts, which are influenced by both logic and emotion. Sometimes we take one tiny logical fact out of context and our emotions blow it up to absurd proportions, applying it to unrelated circumstances and creating disastrous results for ourselves.

Let's look at a common workplace circumstance through a real-life example (with a few minor details changed). Demetrious worked hard at his first job out of college as an Assistant Project Manager, but he could never seem to figure out what his supervisor, Donna, wanted. She constantly criticized him, humiliating him in front of others in the hallways and during meetings. Donna would roll her eyes whenever he spoke and sometimes even talk over him when it was his turn to share information. When it came time for Demetrious's annual review, Donna handed him a Performance Improvement Plan (PIP) with thirty days to improve or face termination. In the days that followed, Donna treated him more harshly than ever, seemingly with the intent of coaxing him to quit before the end of the probationary time frame. She called his work "shoddy" and "unprofessional" and said, "a second grader could do your job better than you." Her bullying technique worked. When Donna asked him to restart a report for the third time over a trivial detail, Demetrious packed up his things and resigned—even though he had twenty days remaining on his PIP.

One might think Demetrious was relieved that he would

never have to step foot in that office or see Donna again. But this was not the case. He just couldn't get past her harsh criticism…

Shoddy. Unprofessional. A second grader could do your job better than you.

These words haunted Demetrious. He took them to heart, considering them as fact. This had been his first job after college, and he didn't have anything to compare it—or Donna's leadership style—against. "I guess I'm an incompetent idiot," he thought to himself. "I'm not good enough for any kind of office job."

I feel for Demetrious and anyone who has ever been in his position. Whether or not he had the capacity to do his job properly or if Donna had failed to provide sufficient training, support, and guidance is beside the point. Donna lacked the leadership skills and empathy to choose her words carefully and avoid crushing this poor young man's ego. She inflicted serious, lasting damage on Demetrious's psyche, which turned bitter and self-deprecating. Instead of letting go, Demetrious convinced himself that he was indeed *a failure*. He had taken a few words, accepted them as fact, attached emotions to them, and allowed them to fester and breed. At twenty-two years of age, after only six months in his first job, he had already developed a negative, hopeless mindset. What a tragedy! He viewed his career as doomed because of one job choice that was a mere speck in what could be a vast, bright future. It's like a puppy who is struck by a broom every time she barks. The next owner might be warm, gentle, and loving to her—but the dog forever after muffles her sounds to whimpers and runs and hides at the sight of anything that remotely resembles a broom handle.

I'm not implying that Demetrious (or anyone) is like a puppy; I make the point only to demonstrate the similarity in muscle memory when it comes to negative influences. Unlike puppies, however, human beings have the capacity to undo and reverse negative programing if they are provided with the right mindset tools to support goal setting. Let's start unpacking a few of them.

The Power of Positive Thoughts

Have you ever had any of the thoughts listed below? Be honest with yourself.

Nothing good ever happens to me.
Why do I even bother trying?
It's too late for me to change or even try.
I'm always messing things up.
Why can't I be like everyone else?
Maybe I'm not cut out for this.
They are judging me.
I'll never be good enough to get that job.
Other people are more qualified and capable than I am.
I screwed up last time, and I'm sure I'll do it again.
I'll probably get another lousy boss in my next job.
I'm sure I'll hate the next job as much as the last one.
I doubt I'll make it through the first year of a new job.
My idea is never going to get off the ground.

If any of the above (or something similar) has ever crossed

your mind, your first order of business is *awareness*: recognizing that the problem exists. It's only when you open your mind, look at yourself in the mirror, and pinpoint the problem that you can start to pivot away from self-detrimental thoughts. This is essential, because if you've accepted certain negative things as fact and associated your emotions with them, the brainwashing has already taken hold and you probably don't notice or believe anything is wrong. You have accepted the chatter in your mind as truth.

Here's the problem: If you believe you will fail, you probably will. Napoleon Hill, author of *Think and Grow Rich,* famously wrote that "thoughts are things." The concept is simple: A universal energy exists that can make our deepest desires come true or realize our worst fears. If we have doubt in our minds, that signal—or a vibration, if you prefer—gets sent out to the universe, which responds: "Okay, I believe you, so that's what will be mirrored back to you."

Science backs up the notion that certain types of thoughts result in the release of different chemicals in the brain. Positive thoughts, for example, lead to increased serotonin production, which causes a state of relaxation and a feeling of well-being. By contrast, negative thoughts trigger stress and anxiety via a flood of cortisol and adrenaline. These hormones are essential for when we face true on-the-spot danger—such as the appearance of a rattlesnake—and our fight or flight instinct kicks in. However, when we have constantly high levels of cortisol and adrenaline shooting through our metabolism, we are subject to a range of greater issues, such as depression, poor memory, bad decision-making, or exhaustion.

In the story cited earlier, Demetrious took in everything Donna said to him at face value and ruminated on it. Not only did the constant flow of cortisol and adrenaline prevent him from trying again and throwing himself back into the job market, it also sent signals out to the world that he wasn't worthy of another position. For these reasons, Demetrious struggled to get responses to his job applications and subsequently failed to impress employers during interviews.

Demetrious needed to single out his prior circumstances and then compartmentalize them in his mind with the positive statement: "It didn't work out, so what? It was my first job. It was a bad fit for me and a learning experience. There are thousands of jobs out there I can do well; I just need to find the right one."

Sometimes it's a serious struggle to compartmentalize, because the self-brainwashing and emotions connected to it are too powerful. Try as you as might, part of your mind continues to project the image of the person that hurt you. A voice in your head jolts you with the words, "But wait—what if she is right about me? What if I end up wasting my time and failing again? I can't stand to face such humiliation again."

Goal Tending

Question: What do you do when negative thoughts impact your ability to accomplish a goal?
Answer: Think backwards!

When you created your vision, you were looking to see what

your dream looked like in its future state. You can do something like this to help overcome negative thoughts and accomplish a single goal.

Suppose your goal is to land a specific job at a certain organization, but you're struggling to find the confidence to apply for it because your last role didn't turn out as planned and the wound still feels raw.

Visualize yourself in the new role one year from now and think backwards: learning all the processes; adapting well to the culture; successfully executing a few projects; and proposing innovative ideas that have been accepted by the organization. Picture a promotion and salary increase, accompanied by a congratulatory handshake from your supervisor.

When you think backwards and break a goal down into small, tangible pieces, you move beyond your challenging past and improve your self-perception of your abilities.

Automatic negative thoughts—known as "ANTs"—are a complete dead-end. The person who caused your pain was probably miserable in her own life and took her troubles out on you. Think about this: Why continue to give this individual such continued satisfaction when she is no longer part of your life? She has probably moved you far out of her sight and out of her mind—and you must do the same.

If awareness, compartmentalization, and seeing your tormentor in a different light don't do the trick, I suggest you try one of more of the following five things:

1. **Start a journal:** Write for fifteen minutes every day—good thoughts, bad thoughts, and everything in between.

2. **Do the tearing exercise:** On separate Post-it notes, write down each negative phase that frequently comes into your head. After you've written them all down, read each one aloud, tear it into shreds, and toss the pieces in the garbage.

3. **Fill the negativity jar:** Every time you have a doubtful thought, put a quarter in the jar.

4. **Send the perpetrator away:** This is obviously a mental exercise, not something to be acted upon. Whenever the words of the negative individual enter your head, step into a private space for ten minutes. Sit in a comfortable position and close your eyes. Take three slow, deep breaths: inhale through your nose and exhale through your mouth. When you feel relaxed, imagine your antagonist in your head saying the harmful words to you. Once you are locked into this image and hear the person's voice, picture them walking further and further away from you into a desert and the sound fading into the wind. Continue to imagine this person until they have vanished into the landscape, and everything is silent. If you continue to see or hear the person, start again from the beginning. Eventually, the perpetrator and the words will both become meaningless to you, like sand blowing in the wind.

5. **Physical exercise:** Physical activity is not only good for your body, it also improves your frame of mind. It doesn't even have to be that strenuous to feel the benefit. Simple things such as walking, biking, dancing, and yoga are excellent for muscles, the cardiovascular system, and brain health. Scientific studies have shown that neurotransmitters such as dopamine, noradrenaline, and serotonin are released during exercise—all of which contribute to a sense of well-being and a stronger physical and mental state.

Even Champions Get Afraid

In the film *Rocky III,* there is a dramatic scene on a beach in which champion boxer Rocky Balboa (Sylvester Stallone) is involved in a shouting match with his wife, Adrian (Talia Shire). The Italian Stallion announces that he wants to quit boxing because he doesn't want to risk losing his family. Adrian called his bluff and presses him to admit the truth, which, after much resistance, he finally does: "For the first time in my life, *I'm afraid!*"

This is no small admittance coming from a tough champion athlete (albeit a fictionalized one) who beat the odds time and time again. If fear can derail Rocky, it has the power to wreak havoc on any of us.

We all fear failure at one time or another. It stands as the biggest obstacle we face while attempting to adjust our mindset. All too often, as in many areas of life, our once courageous career plans go down in a blaze of worry. We become afraid of *what if* scenarios, such as: rejection, financial and psychological risks, and potential embarrassment to family, friends, and peers.

A certain amount of fear is normal. However, it is also one of life's most complicated and debilitating emotions. When faced with a perceived threat—emotional, physical, or both—the brain once again reacts the same way as it does while experiencing negative thoughts, releasing two hormones as part of the fight-or-flight response. I'm sure you already guessed what they are, since I previously mentioned them: cortisol and adrenaline.

If the fear is purely triggered by internal emotions without any kind of visible threat, it is often characterized by others as illogical. This doesn't mean the fear isn't real or has a potentially destructive impact on the mind and body. It can also become a serious threat to one's decision-making ability. Sometimes fear causes us to make rash, foolish decisions. On other occasions, it paralyzes us, and we can't decide at all, which can be just as harmful—especially in terms of lost opportunity.

When we are attempting to do something new and important that is out of the ordinary—such as vie for a high-level position or cold-call a potential billionaire client—we feel vulnerable and afraid. If you are like me and other people have set goals for you, unfamiliar activities that might result in any kind of failure will induce some amount of fear. The reward may be high, but so is the potential repercussion of a misstep.

However, important goals cannot be achieved without facing some level of risk. As poet T.S. Eliot once said, "Only those who will risk going too far can possibly find out how far one can go."

Michael Jordan was perhaps the greatest NBA star of all

time. Did he ever rest on his laurels? Of course not. He constantly challenged himself, setting his mind on attempting all kinds of seemingly far-fetched things, some of which succeeded and some of which tanked. Becoming a baseball player? *Failure.* Majority owner of a basketball team (the Charlotte Hornets)? *Failure.* On the other hand, he made billions from his marketing partnerships: Nike, Hanes, Gatorade, McDonald's, and others. He might not have been nominated for an Academy Award for his performance in the 1996 film *Space Jam*, but he earned $20 million, and fans loved him in it. Plus, getting back to the Hornets, his majority share was $275 million when he started and $3 billion when he sold it thirteen years later (and retained a minority share). So, maybe it wasn't such a failure after all?

My point is that Michael Jordan has proven himself as a risk-taker who is more than capable of moving light years out of his comfort zone. While his genius didn't always translate to success, no one can ever fault him for constantly trying to beat the odds and dispel the naysayers. Jordan was able to overcome his fears because he accepts failure as part of his motivational process to constantly work harder and improve. Despite his myriad accomplishments, he had this to say about his basketball career: "I've missed more than 9,000 shots in my career. I've lost almost 300 games. Twenty-six times I've been trusted to take the game-winning shot and missed. I've failed over and over and over again in my life. And that is why I succeed."

Be like Michael Jordan and take that shot before the buzzer!

Overcoming Your Fear

If you have set S.M.A.R.T. goals, you've already begun the

process of conquering your fears. You're probably asking, "How so?" Remember: The "A" in the acronym stands for "Achievable." If it's already passed your personal bar, then you've established that you have the capability of successfully accomplishing the goal. This means that you can be confident that your skills, creativity, knowledge, and experience will be more than enough to get you past the finish line in good form.

Just after I completed boot camp, one of my earliest Navy leaders, a Master Chief, recommended to our A-school class— the first training school after boot camp, where sailors learn skills related to their chosen field—that we should buy real estate in every place where we were stationed. He said we'd make more money from this than the Navy would ever pay us. Well, it didn't turn out to be an accurate prediction—at least at first.

I took his advice and, without any prior experience, collected a few properties in the Philippines, Hawaii, and a couple of other places. Some properties fared well; others bled money every month. At the time, I would have said my commander had led me astray but, as the years went on, I learned from my mistakes and found the right mentor, who taught me the secret of success in this sector. Eventually, I made more money in real estate than the Navy would ever pay me—something that couldn't have happened if I'd been too afraid to follow my Master Chief's suggestion. It also would never have occurred had I been too scared to try again after my initial disappointments.

To further shift your mindset away from fear, try these techniques:

1. **Admit your fear:** Write down everything that scares you about attempting your goal. Then read the list aloud. What are the worst-case scenarios? Underneath each fear, write down why you are working on the goal. What are the favorable results from achieving it?

2. **Control the controllables:** In a notebook, create two columns: the left is for things you can control as you execute the goal; the right is for the things you cannot control. My advice is to primarily focus on the things listed in the left column, as the ones on the right will happen no matter you do—so why spend any time worrying about them?

3. **Find a trusted coach or mentor:** Find a mentor—someone experienced who will share sage advice, inspire you, give you confidence, and listen to you.

4. **Consider bringing in a trusted partner:** Working with the right partner in any endeavor can be empowering. First, you won't feel alone, which will automatically alleviate some of the burden off your shoulders and reduce your fear. Two heads (and bodies, if that's the case) are already better than one to get the job done faster and better. Each partner would have the other's back to prevent a misstep before it happens. Plus, you have a sounding board to help brainstorm ideas.

A Big and Bold Mindset

My true goal of this book is to unlock the hidden potential that resides within you. You need to believe with all your heart and soul that you will accomplish your goals and win big. Consider the following victorious underdog stories throughout history:

- **David:** The Biblical figure who defeated Goliath.

- **Hannibal:** The Roman army may have outnumbered Hannibal and the Carthaginians nearly two-to-one in the Second Punic Wars (219 BCE-203 BCE), but the underdogs embarrassed them and caused massive—as many as 70,000—losses.

- **The American colonists:** The ragtag Continental Army led by General George Washington beat the mighty British in the Revolutionary War (1775-1783).

- **Andrew Carnegie:** Carnegie's rags-to-riches story is legendary. Born to poor Scottish laborers, he took on his first job at thirteen working in a textile mill, shortly after his family immigrated to Pennsylvania in 1848. He rose up the ranks in the railroad industry and invested his money in several businesses. This brought him enough wealth to create the Carnegie Steel Company, among other businesses, and ultimately become the richest man in the world.

- **The 1969 New York Mets:** The most laughable losing team in Major League Baseball history conquered the seemingly far superior Baltimore Orioles in the 1969 World Series.

- **The 1980 U.S. hockey team:** The "miracle" American team won gold against the favored Russian team at the Olympics in Lake Placid, NY.

- **Erin Brockovich:** In 1996, Erin Brockovich, a divorced and unemployed single mother, took on the juggernaut Pacific Gas & Electric (PG&E) company. She won a $333 million lawsuit against PG&E for contaminating the drinking water in Hinkley, California, where the residents had been suffering from an array of medical conditions.

Al Michaels, announcer during the 1980 Olympic hockey games, asked and answered his own question as the final seconds ticked by in the game between the U.S. and Russia: "Do you believe in miracles? *Yes!*"

Accomplishment of your goal may or may not be a miracle—or require one to occur—but you must believe in yourself as if you were David preparing his slingshot to fire against Goliath. No matter what you think the odds might be or what fears you may be struggling against, you must have completion conviction that you will succeed. This is the mindset of a true champion. Next, I'll guide you on the three mindset shifts you need to make to become a champion yourself.

5

Making the Three Essential Mindset Shifts

"Once your mindset changes, everything on the outside will change along with it."—STEVE MARABOLI

When you hear the word champion, what sports figures come to mind? I'd wager it's one or more of the following people: Michael Jordan, Serena Williams, Mohammad Ali, Michael Phelps, Mia Hamm, Billie Jean King, Lindsey Vonn, LeBron James, Tom Brady, Shohei Ohtani, Patrick Mahomes, or others who have reached the highest level of achievement in their respective sport and sustained it.

The one athlete you would likely *not* cite? Billy Beane, the subject of the bestselling book *Moneyball,* by Michael Lewis, and the 2011 film adaptation, starring Brad Pitt. A high school basketball, football, and baseball star, Beane was an athletic prodigy seemingly on his way toward achieving greatness. His .500 batting average one year on his high school baseball team caught the attention of the New York

Mets, who recruited and assigned him to a Class-A team.

Unfortunately, Beane's professional baseball career never took off, as he flitted from the minor leagues to the majors and then back down again. It seemed as if no matter how hard he tried, he just couldn't hit top-level professional pitching. The consensus was that he had the skills and talent but lacked the mindset of a champion. The greater effort he applied, the worse he performed because he lost confidence in his ability. Deep down, he didn't *believe* that he belonged among the elite players.

Beane turned the page when he became general manager of the Oakland A's baseball team. While in this role, he completely changed his mindset and became a student of data analytics to drive business decisions, which contrasted with the then accepted approach of using emotions or gut feelings to guide recruitment and team strategy. Even though Beane was given one of the lowest player salary budgets in the major leagues, the A's reached the playoffs four years in a row, thanks largely to the general manager's unique algorithmic method. In 2002, the A's won a record twenty consecutive games. Four years later, the team won its first playoff series. Although the A's didn't capture the World Series or even an American League title, Beane proved himself a winner. His data analytics approach revolutionized the way players are recruited, and teams continue to build on his methods to this day.

When I started out as an entrepreneur, I experienced some success when I was younger but couldn't seem to succeed at the next level, much like Billy Beane's struggles as a professional ballplayer. I longed to have my own business or become a high-level director or manager but always came up short. Once I finally broke through that barrier and achieved my goals, I looked back and analyzed how I arrived there. It was an epiphany for me when I identified the power of mindset and the three progressive shifts that I had made that led to my breakthrough success.

In this chapter, I will share insights from my business journey that will give you the necessary mindset to complete your goals and become a champion in your industry.

Mindset Shift One: Believe It Before You See It

You are probably familiar with the team training exercise in which a person falls backwards and trusts that someone will catch them. When it comes to being an entrepreneur or a small business owner, you need to believe wholeheartedly that, if you happen to ever fall backwards, the world will be there to support you.

Neale Donald Walsch, author of *Conversations with God,* wrote, "There are those who say that seeing is believing. I am telling you that believing is seeing." This sentiment doesn't just apply to religious faith. It refers to anything you want or need to accomplish, including your short- and long-term goals. I would take Walsch's concept a step further and say "believing *before* seeing" is the correct mindset shift, as it instills unbridled faith in yourself, bringing clarity to things that are often abstract and converting fear into confidence.

The main issue with the *seeing before believing* concept is that it often leads to the following two self-limiting beliefs:

How do I know I can do it if I've never tried it before?

And, if I haven't seen it before, how will I ever be able to do it?

When I was a teenager working as a dish boy in a local diner, I would study the people in the roles above me to learn about the higher positions in the business. Then, while alone and doing some activity such as watching TV or completing high school homework assignments, I would visualize myself performing the restaurant manager's responsibilities: counting out the bills, opening and closing the diner, scheduling employees, managing inventory, and working with vendors on purchase orders. This worked to my advantage at the time, as I rapidly climbed up several rungs up to assistant manager of the restaurant while still in high school!

The problem with the above scenario was that I was thinking *far too small*. Why did I picture myself as an assistant restaurant manager when I could have been envisioning myself as the *manager* of a restaurant? Or maybe as the owner of a *chain* of restaurants! I didn't reach for the stars, because I was a high school kid at the time, so it didn't even occur to me that I could accomplish these things.

Years later, I did the same thing in a professional setting. When I was an engineer in a nuclear consulting company, I visualized being promoted to a team lead and manager, yet never thought about being a vice president or stock owner. But why not?

There are some people who think about their potential in even smaller terms than I did. They envision themselves performing their current role somewhere else, which, at best, translates to a lateral move. If you don't believe in yourself enough to reach for the stars, you will live the rest of your days wondering why your career never took off from the launch pad. This is precisely why you need to think big and believe with heart and soul that you are capable, worthy, and deserving of achieving your goals and fulfilling your wildest ambitions.

When I was growing up, my Mom used to say to me, "You can do anything if you put your mind to it." This sounded well and good but, when I stepped down from my role as an engineer in corporate America, she—as well as several other family members and friends—cast shadows of doubt on my decision, asking pointed questions like: "Are you *sure* about this?" Suddenly, the concept of my being able to do "anything" only applied to concrete things that could be *seen* and *grasped*.

Despite their good intentions, my family and friends were bringing me down several notches, inadvertently sparking a limited belief within me that hadn't previously existed. I had to find a way to break through this and fully believe that I could accomplish my goal to become a successful entrepreneur. I had to latch onto something that would recalibrate my mindset and get me back on track. A personal preference unexpectedly did the trick....

For as long as I can remember, I've hated waking up early. This was particularly painful for me when I was in the military and had to get out of bed at 5 a.m. to report for duty. Later, when I worked as an engineer and one of our clients was a remote nuclear plant, I had to wake up even earlier to the sound of an alarm and commute to work for over two hours round trip, like millions of people grinding out a workday.

I wondered whether I might somehow be able to channel my loathing of rising early as an incentive to push me forward to starting out on my own. Every so often, I would visualize what a new lifestyle might look like. I imagined myself waking up at my leisure without an alarm. I would then enjoy breakfast at my favorite local restaurant instead of going to work at a company. Since the Navy had denied several of my vacation requests, I pictured being able to take time off and enjoy leisurely travel without having to apply for leave. I focused on these concepts until I believed they were not only possible but were soon going to become my reality.

Once I believed I could succeed as an entrepreneur, I was able to commit to it—and then I started to *see* it. While I can't begin to compare myself to the modern-day tycoons of industry, their belief systems—which led to their unmatched successes—corroborate this theory. Steve Jobs, who co-founded Apple, believed in the potential of personal computing long before it became mainstream. Richard Branson, creator of the Virgin brand and now a pioneer in space travel technology, believed in the value of good customer service years before it became standard teaching in business schools. Mark Cuban, former controlling stake owner of the Dallas Mavericks NBA team and one of the stars on the *Shark Tank* TV show (until 2025), thrives on educated risk taking because he believes in his passion—especially when it comes to banking on emerging technology. These individuals not only had unwavering faith in themselves when they started out and overcame tremendous negativity and obstacles, they took their many failures in equal stride as their successes, learning from their mistakes and carrying on as if they were part of the plan all along.

To overcome self-doubt—especially when it sideswipes you from someone else's negativity that may or may not be well-intentioned—you must believe so vigorously you will accomplish your goal that you are willing to take a necessary leap of faith and potentially risk failure, as leaders such as Jobs, Branson, and Cuban did time and time again. The visual image of your goal in your mind and undeterred belief serves as a powerful ally to help you fill in the unknowns, which decreases your levels of fear and doubt.

There is also a mind exercise you can try that works wonders. If you are about to take a leap of faith to become an entrepreneur or start a small business, answer the following five questions. They may seem like clichés at first but, when you answer them in your mind, you'll find that your responses to them will provide you with unshakeable resolve.

1. How will I ever know if I could do it if I don't even try?

2. What do I have to lose?

3. What's the worst thing that can happen?

4. What's the best thing that can happen?

5. As a fallback, I can always return to my original career if I have to, right?

Mindset Shift Two: Abundance Over Scarcity

I have a friend who knew he was going to be a writer since he was five years old and submitted his stories to New York publishing houses. He spent his whole life writing but supported himself through 8 a.m. to 7 p.m. jobs that were often soul crushing. When he left an executive corporate position in his early fifties, he decided that he had to make a move and dedicate himself completely to building his writing career before it was too late. He developed a business vision and was confident that he had the talent to make it.

The reality set in the first month he set off on his new path. The bills were piling up—the kids, the mortgage, and so on. His wife pressured him to take a full-time paying job, saying, "This isn't working. We can't live like this. Our kids won't be able to go to college. We're going to be homeless." The family hunkered down and cut back on all spending: gifts, dining out, Starbucks, clothing, cable television, and more. Every expense—especially things related to the writer's business, such as books, office equipment, and attending networking events—was closely scrutinized and usually rejected.

The vision, talent, and effort were all there. The writer had mastered the first mindset shift—believing before seeing—but suddenly became mired in the thought that perhaps he had made a mistake and had put his family's security in jeopardy. He wondered whether only single people could risk leading the writer's life. He and his wife had nosedived into a *scarcity* mindset, rather than one of *abundance*.

I completely relate to this, as I grew up in an environment that bred the scarcity mindset. When my brother and

I were kids, my Dad—a military veteran—would periodically line us up at attention a few feet apart. I'm sure his intentions were good as he tried to impart pearls of wisdom to us, which included Newton's laws (not sure why) and various clichés supporting his frugal nature: "Money doesn't grow on trees" and "There's no such thing as a free lunch."

It shouldn't surprise you to learn that my Dad was a CPA who ran a tight ship at home. He kept the monthly budget on the back of a closet door for the whole family to see. The list only included the bare necessities, such as groceries, clothing, and schoolbooks. There was never anything left over for luxuries and rarely was there a spot for dining out.

These surroundings had a profound effect on me. When I went out with my friends, I never ordered any kind of soft drink or juice—just water. I regarded this as a luxury and not worth the expense. I would think to myself, *Why would I waste my money on something as trivial as soda? What if I end up going broke because I've ordered so many things like this?*

I didn't realize it at the time, but my Dad was inadvertently training my family members and me to have a *scarcity mindset*. This means going through life preparing for the possibility that, if you aren't careful, someday you might end up with nothing. In the meantime, you focus on saving money—rather than building wealth—by only buying the bare necessities. It is a difficult and ineffective strategy to try to "save your way to wealth."

Flash forwards several years later to when I was becoming an entrepreneur. Now that I *believed* I could accomplish my goals, I had to overcome my upbringing and make a second mindset shift from *scarcity* to *abundance*. I was able to relax and put things in perspective. Not only did I realize it was essential for me to spend money on attending networking events, but I also concluded that I shouldn't just settle for the "cheap" tickets; I needed the full VIP package. I wasn't splurging for my ego or to treat myself like I was a king; I was paying an essential business expense. I thought to myself, *How much more can I learn by sitting in a more expensive seat? What important people will I get to meet who can become part of my network and help me grow my business? Would I sit next to someone who could increase the likelihood of my gaining knowledge, insight, and wisdom that I wouldn't be able to find anywhere else?*

I likened my choice to being on an airplane. I stood a greater chance of meeting someone influential in first class who might change my life than I would if I were seated in an economy seat on the back of the plane.

I overcame the self-limiting beliefs that "I would never have enough" and "I wouldn't earn enough," developing the mindset that spending money to invest in myself and my business was all part of the process. I became confident that my investments would ultimately lead to greater revenue and profit.

Later, I read *The Seven Habits of Highly Effective People,* in which Stephen Covey introduced his interpretations of the *scarcity mindset* and the *abundance mindset.* In the former, people see only limitations and believe there is a limited available supply of whatever things are desirable to a specific community. They tend to think in selfish terms: "If someone else achieves success, there will be less for me." People who have a scarcity mindset vie for all the credit and compensation resulting from an accomplishment, bristling at the thought of potentially having to share the limelight or reward with others.

By contrast, people with the abundance mindset are confident and secure. They believe that, by directly or indirectly recruiting others—including a business competitor—there will be ample credit and profits available to go around for everyone.

For example, let's suppose a pharmaceutical company is developing a revolutionary new drug that is predicted to have a 90 percent cure rate for a certain type of cancer. It's estimated that it would take them at least three years to produce the missing components and have it ready to launch. They discover that their top competitor already has an abundant supply of those ingredients. If they were to enter a mutually equitable partnership, the drug could potentially roll out before the end of the year. They would save many lives and make money sooner rather than later. This sounds like a win-win, right? Unfortunately, all too many businesses default to the scarcity mindset and choose not to collaborate because they don't want to give up a slice of their pie.

Many entrepreneurs start out with a "bootstrapping" mentality. In principle, the idea is smart: You build your business with as little spending as possible. You don't borrow money or take out loans, which would put you in debt right out of the starting gate. The downside of bootstrapping is that you tend to become frugal to a fault and make decisions that limit opportunities for growth. People who do this often use cheap materials that sacrifice quality or implement low-cost production equipment that is slow and faulty. They also underpay employees, milking every drop of labor out of them until they burn out or find employment elsewhere.

Several years ago, I needed surgery to treat a torn tendon in my ankle. The injury progressively worsened to the point that it was dislocating and could eventually rupture. As a military veteran, I had the option of going to the VA for a free surgery. This could be a no-brainer for many people who don't have insurance options, the financial means, or are just economically minded. My health circumstances weren't nearly as challenging as many other veterans but, at the time, I didn't have much money in my bank accounts. At the same time, I had heard some horror stories about VA surgeons—many of whom were residents attempting their first surgeries—and was concerned that they weren't as capable as traditional hospital practitioners.

I decided to probe the potential surgeon about his experience. "How many surgeries like this have you done before?" I asked.

"As of today—well, *none*," he replied.

He took note of my concern and added, "But there's a backlog ahead of you. By the time you're scheduled, I'll probably have done one or two."

His response didn't exactly instill confidence. I Googled the names of surgeons who had performed ankle surgery on professional athletes. I landed on someone suitable and made an appointment with him. During the examination, I asked this surgeon the same question as the one at the VA.

He didn't hesitate to answer: "Oh, about eight or nine times per week."

Instead of having a scarcity mindset that I should accept whatever was free and easy, I opted to pay out of my own pocket to receive better quality care. I ended up with the most accomplished surgeon available for my procedure—the one who performed it eight or nine times per week—and my ankle turned out as good as new.

Did I suffer from some short-term financial shortfalls afterward? Absolutely. But I had made the decision that it was well worth the risk, because I truly believed the money would come back to me at some point. I didn't think in terms of how little I had in my bank account. I projected outward that what I had done was best for my body and my future and remained assured that someday the money would return to me. Ultimately, having an abundant mindset paid off richly.

I know budding entrepreneurs and small business owners who struggle with this concept. They believe only what is tangible for them in terms of cash in and cash out. At the first sign of trouble—a client refuses to pay for services, an account goes bankrupt, an overhead expense is greater than anticipated, or a make-or-break deal falls through—they can only see and feel the pain and fear of debt, potential bankruptcy, and losing everything. Some throw in the towel, give up their dreams, and return to working for someone else or enter corporate America. The scarcity mindset takes over.

The abundance mindset doesn't mean taking unnecessary foolish risks or making bad business decisions. Nor should a person ignore a serious issue, pretending that it will resolve itself. I'm proposing that one should accept the mindset of abundance and not give up because of one or two gloomy months or a string of temporary setbacks.

The first thing to do is to review your score on the

Self-Assessment in Chapter One and remind yourself of where you stand. If you fell below an 80, take a hard look at yourself and question whether you aren't succeeding in your goals because you are suffering from a scarcity mindset. Below are a few additional telltale indicators:

- Frequent use of the word *hope* in conversations with clients, potential customers, and influencers, as in: "*I hope* to hear from you." This word diminishes your authority and suggests that you aren't worthy of the other person's time.

- You've held back making purchases that could enable you to reach more customers or improve the quality or speed of your performance. For example: Your goal is to be a full-time professional writer, but your monitor is cracked, and your keyboard is missing four keys, yet you don't feel you can afford to invest in a new desktop computer or laptop.

- In your company vision, you state that you want to be the biggest widget provider in your town. Instead of limiting your potential to your town, why not strive to become the biggest widget provider in the state, the country, or the world?

- A competitor has suffered a severe flood that severely damaged its factory, warehouse, and all its inventory. They don't know if they can stay afloat long enough for the insurance company to complete its investigation and determine how much damage it will cover. You happen to have an unused factory and warehouse that they could use in the interim, but you decide you'd rather see the competitor go under rather than take the risk that they will have a comeback and eat away at your profits.

In the original *Karate Kid* film, Daniel Larusso (Ralph Macchio) didn't understand why he was performing mundane chores for his sensei, Mr. Miyagi (Pat Morita), when he thought he was supposed to be receiving karate training. Over and over, Daniel waxed cars, sanded floors, painted fences, and other arduous tasks. Daniel ultimately learned two invaluable lessons: repetitive physical tasks can create powerful muscle memory (which, in this case, form the building blocks of karate), and that he already had everything he needed to succeed.

Affirmations can also accomplish these two important things—but without the physical labor. If you are struggling to overcome a scarcity mindset, choose several affirmations from the list below—or others that you prefer—and recite them several times a day. The repetition of affirmations trains your mind to help you resolutely believe in your full capabilities, which provides muscle memory, confidence, and an abundant mindset.

- I am abundant.

- I was born to be abundant.

- I have an abundant mindset.

- I live a life of abundance.

- I attract wealth to me every day.

- My life is full of wealth opportunities.

- Money continually flows into my life.

Stating the following to yourself at least twice a day will also help swat away your scarcity mindset:

> *Yes, I am aware the problem must be resolved. I may have to think outside the box, ask others for help, and work twice as hard to get through this. It will probably place a tremendous burden on me and my family. But I have faith that we will get through it and the riches will eventually come.*

Renowned financial advisor and bestselling author Suze Orman sums it up best: "Abundance is about being rich, with or without money."

Mindset Shift Three: Positioning Yourself for Success

There once was a young, ambitious filmmaker who was rejected from the University of Southern California School of Theatre, Film and Television three times. That same student idolized director Alfred Hitchcock and sought him out on the set of his final film, *Family Plot*. Although Hitchcock refused to meet him and had him removed as a "trespasser," the tenacious young filmmaker persisted in trying to meet another cinematic legend, John Ford. His dream came true: The legendary, albeit crabby, pioneer of westerns gave the student five minutes of his time, during which he dispensed a few pearls of wisdom before ordering him out of his office.

The young filmmaker? Steven Spielberg, of course. He later captured the entertaining John Ford story in his film memoir, *The Fabelmans.*

You are probably wondering what Steven Spielberg has to do with the third necessary mindset shift, *positioning yourself for success*. For starters, Spielberg never gave up on his dream. He could have listened to the naysayers—the powers-that-be at University of Southern California School of Theatre, Film and Television who rejected him three times or Alfred Hitchcock, who turned him away from his film set—but he pressed on with his goals until he finally gained an acceptance into film school and met another of his heroes (John Ford). The one thing Spielberg knew most of all was that he had to position himself alongside other giants in his industry to glean everything possible to reach the top of his craft.

The lesson is clear: To be able to walk the walk and talk the talk, you must associate with the leaders in your industry. Not only will you learn and grow from their words of wisdom, raise your profile by being in their circle, and gain access to other important influencers, but you will also gradually feel like you belong at their table.

In the film *Good Will Hunting,* Matt Damon plays a janitor

(Will Hunting) at Massachusetts Institute of Technology who happens to be a math genius. Throughout the story, Will is shown carousing with his buddies from Boston's rough South Side. It's clear that hanging out with these lovable losers distracts him, holds him back from perfecting his mathematical skills and building a career, and gets him into some legal trouble (fistfights). Even his best friend, Chuckie (Ben Affleck), recognizes that the kid needs to move away from them to achieve his full potential: "I think, maybe I'll knock on the door, and you won't be there."

It may sound somewhat cruel, but to achieve your goals, you may need to break free from your past to position yourself for success. This sometimes means not spending as much time at the local bar drinking beer and watching football with your high school buddies so you can introduce yourself to people who can take your business to the next level. It's like the adage from motivational speaker Jim Rohn: "You're the average of the five people you spend the most time with." The other four people in your group of five should be much further along and established in their business journeys than you. You want to position yourself in the same circles as the most successful people in your field, so you can learn and grow to your maximum capability.

Some people suffer from impostor syndrome, meaning they feel as if they don't belong among the upper echelon of professionals in their fields. They think they are "faking it" and don't deserve success. They constantly fear being exposed as "frauds."

Trust me: *You are the real deal.* You just need to make the mindset shift to positioning yourself for success. Since you have already made the first two mindset shifts—*believing* and *abundance*—you can accept the fact that you *deserve* to sit at the same table as the elites and then make it happen.

When I started out on my own, I had to frequently remind myself that in prior roles I was always solving major complex problems for other people. This led me to challenge myself with these questions:

If I could do that, why not try to solve my own business problems?

If I were to start interacting with highly successful people, wouldn't I then have an opportunity to help them solve their problems as well?

Once I accepted the fact that I belonged among the top people and could add value for them, I started to think: *Hey, if I can solve a one hundred-thousand-dollar problem for them, I can also solve a million-dollar problem. And, if I can solve a million-dollar problem, I can build to helping them resolve a ten-million-dollar problem…*

I actively researched where the successful people in my field hung out. Since I already had an abundant mindset, I didn't mind if it cost $10,000 for a VIP ticket at an event. This symbolic luxury "glass of soda" was well worth the added expense, as I realized I might connect with billionaires who could teach me invaluable secrets that I would never learn anywhere else. Suddenly, I found myself among wealthy, accomplished people who also freely spent $10,000 because they wanted to hear what *I* had to say. I was treated like a peer because I was confident, had the right mindset, and could help them solve their problems.

By the same token, I wasn't struggling to reinvent the wheel with my own business. I learned from the best who "had been there and done that" and skipped over their mistakes and pitfalls.

Goal Tending

Wherever and whenever possible, you want to find a way to access the movers and shakers in your industry. I refer to this as *proximity to power*. Your objective isn't to be sycophantic but rather to learn things at a higher level in your industry and make connections with the right people. My mentor was one such person. He knew many important people, so it's no surprise that I found the right accountability partner at one of his events. We'll talk more about this in Chapter Ten.

If I had believed what everyone had told me during my formative years—that being an engineer, doctor, or lawyer was the only path to career success—I never would have put myself out there and accomplished my goals. I learned that you don't need to cut corners or save every dollar until you've "made it." You simply step into your greatness and perform. You move at your own pace as you position yourself for success.

My mentor once said to me: "Business is only 20 percent knowledge, skills, and abilities. The other 80 percent is your emotions and psychology." In your normal workday, as you work toward accomplishing your goals, position yourself for success by being in proximity to the most accomplished people in your field. Take them up on offers to stay in touch by phone or Zoom or meet up with them in person whenever it is mutually convenient. Prepare questions in advance for these sessions. You'll find that just being near these people will enable you to soak up three lifetimes of wisdom in a brief period.

Once you make your three essential mindset shifts, you will be well on your way to becoming a full-fledged goal-setting champion. There is only one thing that remains: following my five steps to achieving your goals.

PART THREE

Taking
the
Five
Steps
to
Achieving
Your
Goals

6

Step One—Visualizing the Process

"The only limit to our realization of tomorrow will be our doubts of today."—FRANKLIN D. ROOSEVELT

Now that we've laid the groundwork and established the right mindset, we are ready to tackle the first step in the goal creation process: *visualization.*

We touched on the subject in the last chapter in the section covering the second mindset shift: *Believe it before you see it.* As you'll recall, the intent of that mindset shift was to instill unbridled faith in your capabilities far beyond what you are currently doing, so you can *think big.* Most people set a low bar when they start preparing their goals—as I did years ago—which limits their potential. If you're a star high school baseball player and dream of someday becoming a professional, it's unlikely that your end game is to play for the Savannah Bananas exhibition team. (Not that there is anything wrong with this, the team is quite entertaining!) You want to make it all the way to "the Show"—the major leagues!

What Is Visualization?

Visualization is a simple process to define: It's the act of creating a symbolic picture in your mind of what you hope to achieve and then believing so emphatically in it that you are *willing it to happen.*

When Napoleon Hill wrote that "thoughts are things," he also meant that you could control what reverberates in your mind and send out signals that will be picked up by the cosmic universe, set into motion, and ultimately come to fruition. In Hill's words: thoughts are "powerful things at that, when they are mixed with definiteness of purpose, persistence, and a *burning desire* for their translation into riches, or other material objects."

Winners Visualize

Contrary to some perceptions, visualization isn't a "woo-woo" flaky thing. It's a legitimate technique that has benefitted many people in a wide range of subject areas, including business, sports, and the arts. You might be surprised by the lengthy list of accomplished people who proudly acknowledged that visualization was a major factor in achieving their success:

- **Business tycoons:** Andrew Carnegie (steel magnate), Richard Branson (Virgin), Elon Musk (SpaceX and Tesla), Sara Blakely (Spanx), Steve Jobs (Apple), and Oprah Winfrey (Harpo Productions).

- **World-class athletes:** Michael Jordan (basketball), Lindsey Vonn (skiing), Michael Phelps (swimming),

Katie Ledecky (swimming), Evan Longoria (baseball), Billie Jean King (tennis), Novac Djokovic (tennis), and Roger Bannister (runner).

- **Renowned artists:** Jim Carrey (comedian/actor), Will Smith (actor), Jay Z (rapper), Lady Gaga (singer/actress), Arnold Schwarzenegger (actor/bodybuilder), Denzel Washington (actor), Steve Harvey (TV host), Twyla Tharp (dancer), and J.K. Rowling (writer).

It would be futile to refute the claims of so many accomplished people who attribute their breakthrough success to the power of visualization, especially since at least a few of them tilt toward left-brain (logical) thinking. If it worked for them, what is the harm in giving it a try?

The Science Behind Visualization

When I ventured out on my own as an entrepreneur, I didn't actively follow an existing model for using visualization techniques to successfully complete my goals. I was doing it naturally as well as on the fly, relatively oblivious to all the prominent examples cited earlier in this chapter. I don't know whether my intuition was guiding me or if it was dumb luck, but somehow, I found my way in the right direction. In this section, I will give you the basics on visualization from my own trial-and-error blended with some tips from experts that I discovered after the fact.

The first thing you must do is *accept that visualization truly works*. Again, this practice isn't anything otherworldly that is just limited to mind/body/spirit gurus and their followers. It's like any other deep faith, except that visualization is secular and you can believe in any religion or be an agnostic or atheist and yet still reap its benefits.

Visualization has been scientifically proven. Imagine you are tapping into the energy all around you and tuning in to the frequency that will pay attention to your needs and wants and align them with the universe. Albert Einstein proved that atoms exist, while French physicist Jean Perrin did the same for molecules. We can't see atoms or molecules with the naked eye, but now we simply accept the fact that they are all around us and consist of unique energy. The average human brain contains *seven billion billion billion atoms*—much of which still hasn't been mapped out—so it's entirely logical that it has the power to "dial in" to the signals of outside forces.

The mind/body connection forms a powerful unity that is supported by scientific study. The Cleveland Clinic, for example, found that people who visualized exercising at the gym and then went regularly experienced a 30 percent increase in strength that didn't occur among those who were gym regulars but didn't visualize. In addition, those who pictured themselves going to the gym but never actually went miraculously increased their body strength by 13.5 percent—a benefit not gleaned by people who didn't do any visualization or exercise.

Dr. Joe Dispenza, *New York Times* bestselling author, researcher, and international lecturer, is a proponent of the "power of thoughts"—something of a continuation of Napoleon Hill's "thoughts are things" philosophy referenced at the beginning of this chapter. He believes that we have a choice: Are we going to live according to the "memories of the past" or create a "vision of the future" for ourselves? The latter option is what paved the way for so many great leaders to achieve their breakout success.

If you go to sleep every night trudging up all your current problems and past mistakes and then wake up continuing to ruminate on them, these circumstances become emotional baggage. This baggage then influences your decision-making—which most often involves anxiety and saying "no" to new opportunities because of the risk associated with past challenges that resulted in disappointment. However, if you can use visualization to relax your head at night and again in the morning, you free yourself up to be receptive to a whole new realm of ideas and possibilities.

Dr. Dispenza's approach, which concentrates on meditative practice, involves clearing the mind from the past and stepping outside immediate problems. Once you separate yourself from the emotions of whatever dilemma you might be facing, your brain begins to uncloud. Not only do you focus better, your heart rate improves, and ideas and solutions strike you without effort. (Dr. Dispenza refers to this as "heart coherence" and "brain coherence.") In time, the positive energy from the outside world becomes attracted to you as well. Dr. Dispenza has thousands of case studies of clients at his retreats who began to see significant results—in terms of physical health, mental outlook, and movement toward accomplishing their goals—after only one week. He even helped treat COVID-19 patients using visualization techniques.

In one notable case reported to Dr. Dispenza by Dr. David Hamilton, a woman suffering from severe kidney disease healed herself with daily regimented visualization exercises. Dr. Dispenza explained the science behind how this worked as an effective self-treatment. He describes a process called "mental rehearsal" in which "we are truly present, we are in the moment, and we are visualizing process, the brain does not know the difference between the real-life experience and what the person is imagining. Now, experience enriches brain circuitry. The problem is, when we're facing a health condition or crisis, we always tend to focus on what we don't want to have happen instead of what we do want to have happen because the arousal of the stress hormones prepares us for the worst." By focusing exclusively on the positive outcome, however, "you start to install neurological hardware ahead of the event. Now, if you keep doing it, the hardware becomes a software program, and it becomes easier to do it the next time because you are creating circuitry… you're installing a new mind."

While there is even more science available behind visualization, you don't need to grasp all of it to benefit from the action and convert it into a rewarding routine. I didn't when I started out. Take a leap of faith and give it a try!

Visualization Is Like Playing Chess

I liken visualization to a game of chess. The TV series *The Queen's Gambit* beautifully depicts what goes on in the mind of a young chess prodigy (Beth Harmon, portrayed by Anya Taylor-Joy). When Beth prepares for her chess matches—or even just seeks to improve her level of play—you can see her mental images projected in front of her, such as on the ceiling when she's lying down. Beth isn't simply studying or memorizing, she is *envisioning* dozens of future moves and potential outcomes as if she's already immersed in the match and part of the chess board itself. While some of this is clearly embedded in her innate gift and staggering intellect, she is also taking things several leagues beyond that to ensure victory.

In my case, I learned how to play chess when I was four years old. I started to play competitively and won the Maryland state championship at age nine (via tiebreaker). I continued to enter competitions through junior high school. I was good at it and won my share of matches, although I had no pretense that I could play anywhere near the level of masters such as Gary Kasparov or Bobby Fischer. One thing I involuntarily knew back then—and am even more intentional about now in terms of business goals—is the importance of projecting myself into the game ahead of time.

We aren't talking about simple transactional thoughts: It's not just making the right move and accomplishing the objective. These are important, of course, but it's infinitely more than those things. If you want to land a major account or close a big sale, for example, you must immerse yourself in the moment of making your pitch. This means conjuring up images of yourself successfully delivering your presentation, fielding tough questions with finesse, charming your prospect, and ultimately, getting the other party to sign on the dotted line on an agreement that exceeds your ambitious revenue and profit goals.

The visuals tell only part of the story, however. Your

imagined scenario should trigger as many of the other senses as possible: taste, smell, hearing, and touch. It may sound odd but think in terms of the entirety of what your mind, body, and soul might experience during the important encounter. If you want to someday own a new Lamborghini, for example, you can immerse yourself in the driving experience ahead of time. What does the inside of the car smell like? What does the dashboard look like? What does the engine feel like as you cruise down the highway? All these elements stimulate brain chemistry—notably dopamine (the neurotransmitter of pleasure) and serotonin (the neurotransmitter of happiness)—and form a reality that makes the outcome seem entirely possible.

If you are about to make an important business presentation, for example, here are a few things that might run through your imagination:

- *What are you wearing?*

- *What are the other professionals wearing?*

- *What does the room look like?*

- *What does the room smell like?*

- *Will you drink coffee beforehand?*

- *Might breakfast or lunch be served?*

- *Will you be sitting or standing during the presentation?*

- *Will you share a presentation on-screen?*

- *As you flip through the presentation, are you tapping on a keyboard?*

- *Can you imagine hearing the attendees laughing at your intended jokes and applauding at the end of your presentation?*

The sum of this immersion is that you can feel everything happening in the room ahead of time as if you are in a 3D projection (or artificial intelligence, take your pick) and turning it into an obsession. You want to eat, drink, think, and sleep your visualization and convert it from voluntary to involuntary, so all you think about is the successful realization of the goal. You are conditioning yourself to be ready for the big moment—like Michael Jordan leaping for a basket on the basketball court; Steve Jobs delivering his pitch perfect message about the iPhone; and struggling young pre-fame comic Jim Carrey writing a check to himself for $10 million for his future film career.

You are now ready to make your first move.

How to Establish Your Visualization Practice

The first thing to do is prioritize creating your visualization routine. It's not a "one size fits all" type of thing, but there are certain rules of thumb and minimums of time allotment that should be put in place and considered sacrosanct. Everyone has cramped schedules—especially the elites of every industry, many of whom were cited earlier in this chapter—and yet they all chose visualization as a priority. If you worry that visualization will chew up too much of your time, remind yourself that none of these illustrious champions would have completed their goals and made it to the top without having embedded this into their routines.

Scheduling Time

At the least, you want to block out alone time first thing in the morning and again at night, shortly before going to sleep. When you wake up, your mind is something of a blank slate and open to the power of suggestion without the day's problems getting in the way. In the evening, you are winding down and locking in your thoughts for the day, which means a visualization before sleep can soak into your subconscious, override thoughts of any emotionally draining problems at work, and reinforce the morning's session.

I encourage more scheduled sessions throughout the day, perhaps during a lunch break or later in the afternoon around 3 p.m. If you are feeling particularly overwhelmed, stressed, or negative, a spontaneous visualization time-out can help you recalibrate, refocus, and recharge. There isn't any limit to how many visualization sessions you have in a day; the more, the better—if they are focused on the same scenario to build muscle memory and strengthen your ability to complete your goal.

Amount of Time Per Session

Again, there isn't a hard and fast rule for duration. In the beginning, carve out fifteen minutes for each session and test it out for at least three days. At the end of this span, evaluate how you are feeling and make tweaks here and there as needed. Ask yourself these questions:

- *Is your visualization clear enough?*

- *Is your visualization connecting to your goal?*

- *Are you picturing a big enough outcome?*

- *Is your visualization appealing to all five senses?*

- *Are you feeling positive during the sessions?*

- *Do you feel good afterward?*

- *Do you think you are spending too much or not enough time doing it?*

- *Do thoughts and images from your visualizations come to you throughout the day when you are thinking about or doing other things?*

- *Are you starting to have breakthroughs (new ideas) during or after the sessions?*

As the days go by, continue to evaluate your visualizations and adjust as you go. Don't feel locked into a routine just for the sake of it; each session must work for you and be productive. You can always add or subtract time as needed. For some people, sixty seconds is plenty of time for a productive visualization session.

The main thing is to not allow yourself to become frustrated or discouraged if it doesn't seem to magically work right away. Be patient and set appropriate expectations for yourself. Most of all, don't allow yourself to quit! Michael Jordan never quit—and he would admit to having failed many times—and neither should you.

Your Space for Visualization

You can visualize anywhere you like, if you feel relaxed and comfortable and are free from noise and distractions. Most people prefer a private space where there is little risk of being disturbed. If you are doing it at home, you may have a suitable office or exercise room where no kids or pets will interrupt you.

The workplace can be a bit more challenging. If you have your own office, it's easy to just close the door and lower the blinds. If you don't, perhaps you have access to a small conference room. If your workplace is simply too busy, loud, or public, perhaps you can find a nearby park. Alternatively, you might be able to reserve a room in the local public library if that's convenient for you.

The Visualization Session Itself

It's perfectly fine if you don't aspire to become a mindfulness authority like Jon Kabat-Zinn, Eckhart Tolle, or Deepak Chopra. You don't have to sit cross-legged on the floor and repeatedly chant *om*.

Below are my ten keys to successful visualization:

1. Sit comfortably in your chosen spot.

2. Make sure you don't have distractions; your cell phone must be turned off.

3. Close your eyes and breath in deeply through your nose.

4. Hold the breath for one second.

5. Gradually release the air through your mouth; the exhale should last to a count of five.

6. Repeat steps 1–5 a few times until you feel relaxed, and your mind is completely clear.

7. As you continue with your breaths, recite your positive affirmations of choice. (For a refresher on this, please refer to Chapter 5.)

8. Picture yourself performing the desired action to perfection.

9. Hold onto the image of your action and embellish it with as many of the five senses as you can; immerse yourself in your surroundings until it feels as if you are inside the scenario.

10. Using all five senses, imagine yourself fully experiencing the beneficial result of your accomplished action; this might include money, profit, applause, congratulations, a promotion, or an award.

Repeat the ten steps until the visualization is emblazoned in your mind or your allotted time runs out. When you return for your next visualization, you are duplicating—if not improving upon—the same visualizations with more details and greater clarity.

My visualizations are both scheduled and impromptu. Sometimes visualizations materialize on their own when I'm eating or simply on a break. I welcome them as much as possible since the subconscious mind is always at work and can be unpredictable. You never know when it is trying to tell you something important, so allow it to play out and then listen carefully.

One of my current goals is to find top talent for newly acquired companies to drive those businesses forward. Not only am I looking for individuals with the right skill set, experience, and behavioral profile, I also want to hire people with strong leadership abilities. To accomplish this goal, I spend a lot of time visualizing myself meeting the ideal candidate who has these attributes in abundance. I picture the perfect resume and interview session, as well as the applicant performing the role to a tee. When the time comes for the actual interview process to begin, I know right away if the candidate is a match based on my visualization. I need to feel their energy. If anything seems to be a hair off, I get a queasy sensation in my stomach and then back away. However, whenever my intuition has told me that I've met a strong fit and we end up hiring that person, I'm almost always on the mark. While good luck may have played a factor, I mainly attribute this success to meticulous scrutiny of resumes, asking the right questions, and devoting time and attention to visualization.

It may take a week or two, but with a little patience, you'll discover how multi-purpose and effective visualization can be.

Obliterating Negative Thoughts

Sometimes, despite your best efforts, your mind may not fully cooperate with you. Negative thoughts are evil and often uncontrollable. Every entrepreneur and business owner faces challenges and setbacks—some preventable, others not. It's normal to be harsh on yourself when these things occur, but it's unhealthy to stew on them and even worse to fail to learn from them. If you made a mistake, so what? Acknowledge it, do a proper postmortem to avoid repeating it, and then move on.

If you happen to own properties as I do, you probably feel as if you are always on the cusp of a worst-case scenario. I've gone through catastrophic situations I wouldn't wish upon my worst enemy. Just to give you an idea, I had one tenant who turned a perfectly good residence into a hazardous, unlivable space that couldn't be accessed by anyone without wearing a Tyvek suit (visualize those protective one-piece coveralls used by industrial workers, mechanics, and others who are exposed to harmful elements). The cause? He had a goat living with him!

As a result, the place became so infested with fleas, roaches, and vermin that anyone brave enough to enter without the suit risked being inflicted with a mighty unpleasant rash or series of bites.

Every time one of these awful situations occurs, it feels like a punch in the face or gut. I won't sugarcoat it: It hurts. However, once I've dealt with the issue, I erase it from my memory.

I don't let it haunt me, even if I've lost a lot of money. It's especially important that I don't allow thoughts of mishaps to invade my visualizations. They must be completely tuned out. I imagine it's much like how champion boxers, such as Mike Tyson and Evander Holyfield, took all kinds of punishing blows in the ring at one time or another yet managed to ignore the pain as if it didn't exist and then battle on.

If other types of negativities—such as the unsupportive voices of friends, family, bosses, colleagues, or other critics—creep into your mind, drown them out and replace them with your visualization and accompanying five senses. The more you visualize, the weaker those voices become.

Let's Kick It Up a Notch

Champion Olympic swimmer Michael Phelps has been an emphatic advocate of the visualization process. This shouldn't be surprising, as it has guided him toward winning an astounding twenty-three gold medals, twice as many as the number two athlete on this list. Yes, Phelps is an outstanding physical specimen. He undoubtedly had access to the most cutting-edge training methods, as well as one of the finest coaches (Robert

Bowman) in the world. Of course, Phelps was also fully dedicated to perfecting his skills and put in the time and mental and physical exertion necessary to becoming the best competitor possible.

These factors contributed a great deal to Phelps' unparalleled success, but they are not the only reasons why he won so many coveted awards in his illustrious career, which included snagging an unprecedented *eight* gold medals in 2008. He incorporated a special edge into his visualization process. With guidance from Coach Bowman, Phelps visualized his goal— winning eight gold medals—hundreds of times throughout the day. He pictured every movement, stroke, and turn as if they were utter perfection. He imagined claiming the medals and the celebrations afterward. Then he added an extraordinary, counterintuitive piece to his regimen: He visualized *what might go wrong* during the competition—including solving the problem in the moment without a hitch.

Can you guess what happened? In the middle of the 200-meter butterfly final at the 2008 Olympics, a worst-case scenario occurred: Phelps' goggles began to leak and fill with water. This is a total nightmare for an Olympic swimmer, as it becomes impossible for them to see anything. Essentially, Phelps was swimming blind and couldn't even make out the edge of pool for his turnaround. Instead of panicking, however, his mind went straight to his visualization, enabling him to overcome this challenge and press on without skipping a beat.

One might say that Phelps accomplished something akin to a Jedi mind trick from *Star Wars,* but this was not the case. Bowman and Phelps recognized that anyone could succeed at accomplishing a goal using visualization techniques. The secret, once again, involves creating the goal; tuning out the doubters; repeating the visualization hundreds of times; and, most importantly, focusing on both the desired and negative outcomes, especially imagining yourself seamlessly resolving the problems the split-second they materialize. While the human body must ultimately do the work, all the physical training in the world won't be able to overcome a mental state that is unprepared or in crisis mode. Visualization solves all that and more.

Focus on Your Team, Too

There is one last creative visualization inspired by Michael Jordan that not only benefits you but also raises the chances of the entire organization achieving its desired results. In Game Six of the 1993 NBA finals between Jordan's team (the Chicago Bulls) and the Phoenix Suns, Jordan was shut down by Charles Barkley. This was a rare occurrence that almost signaled the end of the Bulls' reign as NBA champs and would have prevented them from their third consecutive victory. Jordan could have continued to press his offensive skills but didn't because he knew Barkley had his number that day. Instead, the Bulls shifted the strategy and, in the final seconds of the game, Jordan passed the ball to John Paxson, who nailed a three-pointer and sealed a 99-98 win.

Goal Tending

Since visualization is such a powerful tool, why keep it to yourself? Your team can benefit from it, too! At a mutually convenient and comfortable time and place, share your visualization techniques with members of your team. Make sure to cite the science behind it and mention its countless benefits—especially ones you've gleaned yourself, along with the results.

If your team consists of a half dozen members or less, you can even try a group visualization session. This can create some bonding and synergy, especially in terms of being able to relate to everyone's goals and motivations.

One word of caution: Don't make it mandatory or try to "guilt" people into joining the group. If you do, they'll have a predisposition to be suspicious of the activity and perhaps even be negative about it.

Michael Jordan didn't just visualize himself as the hero, he also saw himself as a team player. This type of selfless big-picture collaboration builds camaraderie and team spirit. After that game, who wouldn't want to be on the same team as Michael Jordan? He did whatever was necessary to get the job done—and you should, too. Always consider how visualizing yourself assisting team members might be another weapon to add to your arsenal.

Now that we have delved deep into the recesses of the mind

and established a powerhouse visualization routine that aligns with goal setting, we are ready to shift outward to step two and seek expert counsel.

7

Step Two—Seeking Counsel

"Tell me who your heroes are, and I'll tell you who you'll turn out to be."—WARREN BUFFETT

Sometimes it seems as if everyone is pretending to be an expert on everything and is more than happy to impart advice to you, whether they know what they are talking about or not. Scrolling through social media feeds makes them summa cum laude authorities, right?

Suppose you're writing a novel and excitedly reveal the premise to your hypothetical brother—whose opinion you respect on most things—to gauge his opinion. He says, "Oh, I don't know. Would anyone be interested enough to buy that? Is it worth so much of your time?"

Such words from someone so close to you will no doubt sting and deflate your motivation for continuing to progress with the novel. And yet, your brother's off-the-cuff remarks should have absolutely no bearing on your work; this so-called "advice" should be swatted away like a swarm of gnats. Why?

Because he doesn't know what he is talking about. He hasn't bought or read a book since he graduated from college two decades earlier. He doesn't understand what's involved in writing one or have a clue as to what drives interest or sales. He may be a smart guy and know many other things at a respectable level, but he's not an authority on the craft of novel writing (or even the audience for your novel). This means you shouldn't in any way regard him as counsel or give him space to say a single word about your work.

A similar thing may be said if you were learning how to play golf. Your eighty-year-old Aunt Rosie who golfs twice a week and always has the best score among her retirement community friends might be an excellent place to start to impart to you the rules of the game and perhaps suggest golf equipment and accessories you might need. However, if your goal is to learn how to become a *good golfer*, you want to search for the best instructor or golf pro you can find (and maybe your Aunt Rosie can help point you in the right direction here as well).

Characteristics of a Good Advisor

You must set the highest bar possible as you make your selection. Depending on your needs related to your goals, the expert should meet some or all the following background criteria:

1. Appropriate degrees or credentials (if applicable)

2. Many years of relevant firsthand experience with insider knowledge

3. Regarded (currently, or in the not-too-distant

past) as a "doer" with the right skillsets

4. A record of proven results

5. High stature and good reputation in your industry

6. A wide network of useful professional contacts

7. A schedule that can accommodate time for consultation

At the same time, your advisor should be the "complete package" in terms of style and skillset:

1. Strong intelligence coupled with receptivity to innovative ideas

2. Solid listening skills

3. Direct, concise communication style that includes specific direction or examples, as needed

4. Ability to impart "tough love" without being hyper-critical or condescending

5. Responsiveness and reliability

If you still require a bigger picture of what your counsel looks like, think in terms of iconic film mentors, such as Obi-Wan Kenobi and Yoda (to Luke Skywalker in the *Star Wars* films); Professor Dumbledore (to Harry Potter in the Harry Potter films); and Mr. Miyagi (to Daniel in the *Karate Kid* films). You could also count Rocky Balboa (to Adonis Johnson in the *Creed* films); although the former Heavyweight Champion isn't the sharpest tool in the shed, he fits the other criteria, especially experience, skillset, and track record.

The Navy Way

Like all five of my goal-setting steps, seeking counsel is something I unknowingly practiced but didn't formalize until much later. I was fortunate to have benefitted from expert counsel during my time in the service, as the Navy offers a mentoring program for fresh recruits. In fact, experienced Navy leaders are *required* to advise the newbies about training, policy, benefits, and other areas related to service. Many Navy leaders also go above and beyond and help mentees on personal matters, including their finances.

In my case, my ability to move on from the Navy was inspired by a Navy Master Chief—a former Senior Enlisted Leader—who acted as a counselor to me and my A-school class just after boot camp. He offered advice on how to enter the world of real estate investing, suggesting that we purchase homes wherever we happened to be stationed. As someone who was so regimented by others for my entire whole life, owning real estate symbolized freedom to me, and I eagerly followed his recommendations (although it took three years for them to kick in, since I was only eighteen at the time). I invested in homes in various places—including Seattle, Hawaii, and the Philippines—which helped me learn the basics. From a financial standpoint, it was a mixed bag: Some months I had positive cash flow, while in others I was breaking even or losing money on real estate. I knew I still had a long way to go in my education.

The important thing I have since gleaned about my relationship with the Navy Master Chief is how many strong characteristics of a good advisor he had: years of relevant firsthand experience with insider knowledge, a "doer" with the right skillsets, and a record of proven results (several profitable properties). He may not have had all the qualities I would eventually require—which you should, too—but I was fortunate enough to have him in my formative stages in this new field.

Building the Network

As I mentioned in an earlier chapter, upon leaving the Navy, I became a consultant in the nuclear engineering field. In this role, I worked long hours and traveled so often that I felt like I was still in the Navy. There was no work-life balance for me, as everything was focused on production. I was constantly on the edge of burnout. On top of that, I felt a great deal of stress because it was common for contractors to be laid off or terminated. Real estate served as something of a safety net of passive income and as a beacon of hope to me that someday I might get some relief from the never-ending corporate grind.

I established personal goals of increased financial and social freedom and realized that being an engineering consultant wasn't going to be part of that vision. I had an itch to improve my efforts as a real estate investor but recognized that I had a lot more to learn to become successful, especially since the profession is complex and full of unexpected circumstances. It required a different skillset from anything I had ever studied. I was also interested in expanding to the world of raising capital for real estate investing, which was a whole other ball of wax for me.

At the time, I didn't know a lot of authorities specializing in real estate investing, but I had to start somewhere and approached a bunch of people I knew who were in this line of work, starting with the uncle of a former college roommate who had several rentals. They helped me buy my first couple of houses in the early 2000s, so I am appreciative of their good intentions. The reality, though, is that their knowledge alone would not be enough to get me to financial freedom. I was looking for tactics that could build on the basics and take me to the next level. I started to realize that my current mentors had their hearts in the right places but were not fully in the know. Their philosophy was that "negative cash flow is okay" because it offers great tax benefits and appreciation was the goal. As I later learned, cash flow is far more important than appreciation when one is looking to master real estate.

It was eye-opening to me when I discovered that there were people out there who were almost always making lucrative returns in real estate investing. They weren't just buying something, holding it, and barely making money, but rather, consistently bringing in strong earnings each month.

To help you attain your goals sooner than I did, I'll admit my mistake at the time: I failed to seek counsel who had the right level of expertise with proven results. If you want to be financially free, you must find a mentor who has already reached that level of success (#2 and #4 from my earlier list of criteria). The problem remained that the experienced advisors I needed were outside my network. I had to identify them, figure out where they were and how to approach them, and break into their circle.

To broaden my network and find the right counsel, I attended events held by legitimate real estate investor groups, where I hoped I would be in *proximity to power.* (See Chapter Five for a refresher on this.) At these gatherings, you'll find accomplished sponsors and educators who teach group lessons on real estate, some of whom also offer private coaching for a fee. (You also need to be on the alert against scam artists, which I warn about later in this chapter.) I set my sights on one guy who seemed to be well-versed on real estate and enjoyed talking about it. His knowledge and experience—over three decades' worth—were a cut above any of the other speakers I'd heard up to that point (and since then, too). I went through my criteria, and he passed with flying colors.

I became determined to recruit him as my mentor. My investment of time and money attending that event ultimately paid me back many times over. During my first year working with him, I purchased seven profitable houses, compared to the paltry three I'd bought on my own in the entire ten years prior.

Sometimes it's tempting to chase after the first credentialed mentor you might come across because they have seemingly achieved breakout success and became a millionaire overnight. That isn't necessarily the best game plan, however. Probe deeper. Newer real estate educators that you find on the Internet, for example, may only have three years of results to brag about or stopped doing the activity they are teaching. An even worse scenario would be that they are educating because they were lousy practitioners.

Always check references. It is exceptionally important to verify long-term experience and speak to successful past students, as this vetting will help you determine whether the mentor's advice is sustainable *and* enabled clients to weather economic downturns. My mentor had a much higher level of understanding of how to survive and thrive even when things go bad (which they inevitably do in every industry, and real estate is far from an exception). A good mentor will teach you how to position yourself to navigate ups and downs, which will always be part of the game.

My mentor gave me a much-needed strategy to handle a failing rental property I owned in Hawaii that I had bought when I was stationed at Pearl Harbor. Not only was the property underperforming with only a couple of hundred bucks of positive cashflow, but I also couldn't sell it because the country was going through a recession at the time. My mentor drilled into me a point that I have never forgotten: Every property must have monthly cash flow or else be discarded. The earnings on the Hawaii property were so meager that the property fell into this bucket, and it had to be cut loose.

My mentor showed me how to convert the underperforming asset into a new one with significantly higher returns. With his guidance, I tapped into the 1031 tax exchange—a tool that allows investors to exchange an investment property for another like-kind property and defer paying capital gains tax on the profit earned from the sale, but with a less common twist. I ended up exchanging the single underperforming property into three houses with substantially higher cash flow. By trading one weak asset for three better producing ones, I suddenly went from barely breaking even to earning $2,000 more every month without contributing another dime to the investment. How's *that* for proof of the benefits of mentorship!

Watch Out for Grifters

Unfortunately, for every one upright, devoted, and brilliant advisor, there are three posers who are looking to make a quick buck at your expense. Sometimes expertise is offered with a result that is implied or even promised ("Triple your revenue in three months—guaranteed!"), although not always delivered. This is certainly the case in real estate investing, where there are thousands of professionals and companies claiming to have the secret to turning a small investment into mountains of cash.

There are myriad ways to effectively vet your potential

mentor. Traditional methods include what we normally do when performing any kind of due diligence: *research*. In addition to the criteria spelled out earlier in this chapter, I would advise scrutinizing wherever possible for client/customer reviews, testimonials, or samples of prior work. Interviews with past mentees is always a good idea. Once those hurdles have been cleared, it converts to a recruitment process, starting with the all-important interview.

As an engineer, it's easy for me to detect when someone is an expert by how they respond to questions; their answers should be detailed, thought out, and logical with sources. Identify what hints suggest a person's authority (or lack thereof) in your specific field and be on the lookout for those.

When meeting with a mentor candidate—whether in person, via Zoom, or on the phone—I search for *authenticity* to their words. I probe for answers to these questions:

- *Do they give direct answers to questions or hedge around them?*

- *Are they truly at the expert level or just spouting b.s.?*

- *Are they meeting me where I am in my business?*

- *Is there any hint of condescension or being judgmental?*

- *Are they providing specific examples to support claims?*

- *How do they impart criticism?*

- *Do they sound supportive and inspiring?*

- *Can I visualize conferring with them on a regular basis?*

- *During the conversation, do they sound attentive and genuinely interested in client progression?*

- *Are they respectful while discussing stories involving other clients?*

- *Do they respect confidentiality of other clients?*

- *Do they have gravitas backing up stated experience, knowledge, network contacts, etc.?*

You want to ensure that your mentor knows a lot more than you do and won't hold back in terms of sharing insights that can benefit you. If there is the slightest whiff of competitiveness or jealousy, you'll want to head in the opposite direction.

When possible, in-person interviews will inform you the most. This is when you should look to evaluate these behaviors. The list below is just a guide and not intended as the "end all be all." Mentors do vary a bit from one industry to another.

- *Did they come prepared to the meeting having done at least some background research on you?*

- *Did they ask quality questions to accurately assess your situation?*

- *Did they have good eye contact with you throughout?*

- *Are they taking notes in some way?*

- *Do they seem to be patient during the process or fidgety and in a rush?*

- *Are they doing too much of a sales pitch?*

- *Are they kind and respectful to others in the vicinity—such as a barista (if you are meeting in a coffee shop), a waiter (in a restaurant), or an intern/assistant/receptionist (in the office)?*

Lastly, you'll want to ask for two or three client references. If they can't provide client reference, you know your answer. During the reference checks, you want to validate everything you've gleaned from the research and interviewing you've done. Generally, the former mentee clients will be more than happy and excited to recommend the person who helped them accomplish their goals and share favorable attributes and stories. If the answers are curt or evasive, you know something is awry.

Now we get to the million-dollar question: Should you pay for a mentor? If the person is so rich and successful, why would they even require a fee? On the other hand, everyone should be compensated for their valuable time, especially someone who coaches for a living and when it is their primary source of revenue. There is also the logic that, if they aren't charging you, do they have skin in the game with your outcome?

There is some mixed information on the Internet about this. Paid coaches often get a bad rap, but that's because there are so many who aren't worth their exorbitant fees. Then there are those who offer free sessions but have hidden costs down the road.

The reluctance to pay for expert counsel is understandable, but sometimes you must look at the bigger picture and go for it. The mentors who made the most significant difference to me were well compensated. I believe in the process so much that I subsidized mentor fees for some of my partners.

If the person checks off all the boxes outlined in this chapter and can prove the ability to take your business from a startup to six figure earnings or even beyond, then you have your answer. Isn't it worth paying someone to accelerate bringing you closer to achieving your goals—especially if you are missing important pieces and stagnating? As Ben Franklin said, "An investment in knowledge pays the best interest."

Once your advisor is aboard, you are ready to advance to Step Three—which, ironically, means *working backwards*. Don't worry—it's an invaluable part of achieving goals that won't add even a fraction of a second to executing your strategy.

8

Step Three—Working Backwards, Setting Targets

"Begin with the end in mind."—STEPHEN COVEY

Ancient Chinese philosopher Lao Tzu once said, "The journey of 1,000 miles begins with a single step."

According to Tzu and most conventional wisdom that has since followed, one must always move forward when working toward accomplishing something. The idea is to *make progress* and always advance ahead.

Generally speaking, "going backwards" is not a desirable direction to be headed. No one wishes to lose a major client or suffer a decline in growth or profit that takes you several steps back to your status from a couple of years earlier. These unintended circumstances—whether triggered by uncontrollable outside forces or by a misstep in decision-making—can be frustrating and painful, especially when there aren't any major lessons or improvements to be gleaned from them.

Yes, I completely understand all this, so let's set it aside. Instead, let's focus on intentionally strategizing your plans backwards from the desirable result to its origin, as this is an invaluable way to make tangible progress toward accomplishing your goals.

Reverse Engineering

When you work backwards, you are building on the work you already accomplished based on previous chapters of this book. By starting with a crystal-clear vision of the desired end state and success criteria, you develop clarity of mind and purpose because you know exactly where you want to go, as well as what each stage looks and feels like ahead of time.

By laying out your steps from Z to A instead of A to Z, you begin to dissect and fully comprehend the actions that are required to complete the goal. Not only does it confirm that the last step as important as the first, it also helps you internalize that the goal is real and will be accomplished.

I have been incorporating working backwards into my personal goal setting for many years. Unbeknownst to me when I started, Amazon's product development team developed the same unique concept ("the Amazon Method") with remarkable success. It's hard to argue about the Method's effectiveness, since the company is worth $1.87 trillion as of this writing. Amazon formalizes commencement of a new initiative by generating an internal-only press release announcing the final product as if it's already been created. In this way, the development team can focus efforts on the product's benefits, as well as its features.

You might be surprised to learn that the U.S. Navy has been doing something along these lines for a long time as well, except they refer to it as their official "Navy Planning Process." For major missions, such as evacuating an area devastated by a natural disaster, the planners start with what they refer to as an "end state" tied in with the vision. They identify and then analyze various courses of action (COAs) that lead to the end state. This involves many variables, such as the risk of lost personnel, money, equipment, time, and political collateral. They often wargame each COA, which essentially means mapping out potential outcomes like a chess game to help evaluate the positive and negative consequences of each scenario. Once the best direction has been selected, they sequentially work backwards to anticipate any possible circumstance that can go wrong and then course correct it ahead of time.

Working Backwards as an Investor

I was first introduced to the practice of working backwards by my mentor when I was a fledgling real estate investor. Before then, I had been investing randomly without any real course of action. I was working hard, as I always did, but there wasn't a specific strategy behind my efforts. I would send out offers without much rhyme or reason, other than knowing that this is what real estate investors are supposed to do. I had some hits along with the misses and made some money, but the financial rewards weren't remotely close to what I had in mind.

My mentor put the kibosh on my game of slapping mud against the wall and seeing what would stick. He was strong when it came to real estate investing and strategy, smoothly guiding me through the logical stages of his process:

1. Create your vision and then visualize it.

2. Establish your goal.

3. Work backwards from your goal.

4. Itemize actionable steps necessary to complete the goal.

5. Set your targets.

I was determined to emulate my mentor's success, so I followed his instructions to the letter. He explained that, if you have a financial goal—in my case, generating income that would allow me to retire from serving another entity and become my own full-time boss—working backwards is a particularly effective strategy.

The first thing I had to do was document my existing results. Once I'd done so, I gleaned several vital statistics that informed me on how many offers on average I sent out to calculate my current conversion rate. Next, I ran some projections. I determined that, if I were to send out x number of offers, I would seal y deals (based on my historical conversion rate that I calculated) and thereby earn z revenue. In this way, I could work backwards from my target financial goal and determine how many offers it would take to get there based on my established success rate.

Below, you can view this in simplified hypothetical terms with $100,000 as the annual goal:

Outreach to 2,000 prospects results in 20 people interested, which costs $0.70/outreach

20 interested people/2,000 people in the campaign = 1% response rate

20 offers responding to the interest on average results in one finalized deal ($1.50 cost/offer)

1 finalized deal generates $10,000 in revenue

1 deal/20 offers = 5% conversion rate

$1,430 spent to make on average $10,000 is a 7x multiple

If a target revenue goal is to make $100,000 to replace a salary, 200 offers would need to be made to close 10 deals to reach $100,000.

If each outreach costs $0.70 and each offer costs $1.50, then $14,300 in marketing would yield $100,000.

Final Equation: 200 offers/52 weeks in a year = 3.85 or about 4 offers per week.

In short, how did I make my real estate investing goal from working backwards? By using the above formula as a model, I could deduce exactly how many offers I would need to make per day, per week, and over the course of a full year to my financial goal. It forced me to monitor my pace, no matter what else might be going on. My total number of offers per week had to be on track; if I were to fall short one week, I would be forced to make it up on another.

The working backwards method can work for any type of business. If you own a flower shop, for example, you might look at the conversion rate based on floral varieties. You might also determine what activity (e.g., advertising) generates the sales. On average, if you spend $10,000 per year in advertising to generate $30,000 in revenue, then it stands to reason that you'd need to spend $100,000 to earn $300,000. Or you could test a different type of campaign or marketing method to see what the conversion factor is and then scale accordingly.

The same process would apply to a business consultancy. If you advise fifteen clients per year to generate $500,000 in revenue, you need to double your clientele to thirty—or some other tactic, such as raising fees and/or increasing your offerings to each client—to reach a target goal of $1 million.

Let's use a different example that relates more easily to everyday life. I have a neighbor who sets a goal of reading at least five pages every evening. This works for him because it's such an easy target, even on days when he is exhausted or doesn't have much time to spare. If you multiply five pages per day times 365 days a year, that's over 1,800 pages in one year (or the rough equivalent of seven books). On most days, he reads more than five pages, which leaves him with a feeling of accomplishment and gives him a chance of completing even more books.

Goal Tending

I f you are an avid TV viewer of crime films or television shows, you're already aware that homicide detectives always work backwards when trying to solve a murder case. They are presented with the literal end—a corpse—and must work the trail backwards, examining the evidence at the crime scene, interviewing witnesses, searching for potential motivation, and so on.

Edgar Allan Poe, inventor of the detective story and lauded poet ("The Raven"), understood this concept well and even elaborated on it in his 1846 essay "The Philosophy of Composition," in which he wrote: "Nothing is more clear than that every plot, worth the name, must be elaborated to its denouement before anything be attempted with the pen. It is only with the denouement constantly in view that we can give a plot its indispensable air of consequence, or causation, by making the incidents, and especially the tone at all points, tend to the development of the intention."

Follow Poe's advice in your goal setting, and you are certain to achieve killer results!

It all comes down to a numbers game, where you look at the amount that you want to achieve and then work backwards to see how many offers (or whatever the case might be) it would take reach that mark. Simply substitute the metric or activity that suits your goal. Once you've run the numbers, it becomes a matter of tracking your results regularly to ensure you are following through and executing your strategy. For this reason, it's all right for you to factor in a percentage to anticipate potential failure. No one hits the basket every single time, which means you need to take enough shots as needed to meet your goal.

Setting Realistic Targets

Now let's get down to the nitty-gritty: setting your targets.

When you enter this stage of goal setting, you want to challenge—but not overextend—yourself. There are two sand traps that people often fall into, and they are equally as extreme and dangerous.

The first is establishing a target that doesn't add up to your goal. Always triple check your math and all your assumptions about what is realistic and achievable.

The second involves setting the bar too low, which inevitably means that you will achieve less than your full potential. This is a tragedy, because you end up missing low-hanging fruit and will probably have regrets later that you could have done much better.

The third pitfall is the exact opposite: overdoing it. If the targets are so demanding that you start missing them right away, you begin to get frustrated with yourself and second-guess everything. As time passes and the shortfalls add up to a significant gap, you became even less productive and start asking yourself, "What's the point? I'm never going to make it anyway."

Remember: Your vision or end state should be *huge*. The goals you need to accomplish to achieve this vision should cause you to bend a bit, but they must be realistic and mathematically add up to your desired end state. Don't carry the cliché "Your eyes are bigger than your stomach" from childhood into adulthood. If you work so hard to try to achieve an unrealistic goal that leads the point of exhaustion and helplessness, you'll end up feeling overwhelmed and throw in the towel. In addition, you want to keep your stress and anxiety at reasonable levels and not overtax your physical or mental health. If you get sick or have a breakdown, you'll be out of commission and then certainly won't be able to achieve your goals.

Expect the Unexpected

We all have our good days and bad days. If you don't plan for the latter, you may end up stringing together several consecutive days of missed targets. This will cause a negative chain reaction. You'll get thrown off your game, lose momentum, and never hit your goal. This is what often makes people quit. When we find that we're falling behind and dug ourselves into a deep hole, the natural response is to give up. The key is to set realistic targets that factor in the human element to avoid this situation.

Setbacks, obstacles, and derailments aren't just possibilities. Uncontrollable things go awry all the time. It's simply the way the world turns. For example, if another real estate bubble inflates and then implodes like in 2008, the world of real estate investing—including myself—will be forced to pivot.

You must expect that at least some problems are *guaranteed* to arise throughout the course of a year. In 2023, for example, the Hollywood writers' strike lasted 148 days—followed by an overlapping actors' strike—which meant an extended shutdown of many TV and film projects. During this time frame, dreams were shattered and many people working on and off the set suffered tremendous financial hardships.

You should always have Plan B at the ready, so you are prepared for any worst-case scenario. This doesn't contradict my recommendations from Chapter Six regarding the power of visualization. Smart planning and good preparation don't mean that you are projecting bad things and thus causing them to happen. All boats are pre-stocked with life preservers, just in case something unexpected might occur. The presence of the life preservers onboard the vessels doesn't mean that the boat is going to get caught in a tsunami and capsize. But you sure want them there if you get into trouble.

In the Navy, we always trained to the max and were taught that in battle or stressful conditions we default to the level of our training. As Zig Ziglar famously said, "Expect the best. Prepare for the worst."

Always Chip Away at Your Targets

To consistently meet your targets, you must also be mindful of your time. Look at your day objectively and determine what can realistically be accomplished during your waking hours. How much time can you carve out for this specific daily activity that doesn't negatively impact other aspects of your life?

Your intent is to chip away at your targets to create a sense of consistency and continuity. By doing this, the tasks become second nature and you gradually improve at them, producing faster and better results without having to exert more time or energy. By engaging in repetitive actions, you generate positive momentum that helps offset your bad days or perhaps even complete your goal ahead of schedule.

I have a friend who has a regular exercise routine. His goal is to head to the gym every single day and time he scheduled himself to go, even if he's not physically up to it and just puts his foot in the front door. This might seem silly, but the reality is that it keeps his routine intact. As we all know, the hardest part of any gym exercise plan is *going there and showing up*. Missing one gym session can lead to skipping a second one and then a third, fourth, and fifth. By keeping the continuity going, you prevent the "infection" from spreading. It's also possible—as my friend attests—that, once he's inside the gym, he figures, "Oh, what the hell. I'm here already, I might as well do *something*." And, of course, performing some physical activity is always better than doing nothing at all.

Legendary novelist Ernest Hemingway (*Old Man and the Sea*, *For Whom the Bell Tolls*, *A Farewell to Arms*) coaxed himself to write every day by setting a minimum quota that was always achievable: "All you have to do is write one true sentence. Write the truest sentence that you know."

Successful writers tend to be exceptional target setters. Earlier in this chapter, I cited how difficult it is for some people—such as my neighbor—to set enough time aside just to read books. With that in mind, try to imagine how difficult it is to *write* one (as I am doing here).

Like many creative artists, writers tend to work alone toward accomplishing their goals. I've asked many of the ones I know how they finish writing their manuscripts, and the answer inevitably comes back the same: "I sit myself in my chair every day for however long it takes to get it done."

This isn't just from the perspective of accumulating word count but also from being thoroughly immersed in the work's narrative. The daily routine is such an integral part of the writers' lives that the generation of ideas becomes constant and not relegated to when they are in their chairs facing the computer or laptop screens. The ideas come to them while they are showering, eating, drinking, sleeping, exercising, or performing any one of a thousand other mundane activities. When they return to their desks, the words flow from the subconscious "writing" that occurred during their non-work hours.

It doesn't matter if your work involves writing fiction, investing in real estate, competing on a playing field, caregiving, fundraising, creating computer software, educating, selling shoes, dressmaking, or any other occupation or craft. The process is still the same once you've created your goals and worked them backwards: You must establish goals that push you to perform at your best and doable targets that won't wipe you out. Chip away at your targets every day to keep the momentum going and cumulatively make tangible progress toward completing your goal.

Once you've mastered the target, you can begin to find ways to challenge yourself and grow even more. You may even be able to afford to recruit people to multiply your opportunities, as I did. When I was able to hire and train other professionals to make real estate offers full time, I discovered it was possible to exponentially beat the target I had assigned to myself because I was multitasking on so many things.

To prepare for Step Three, we can take some goal-setting inspiration from the Godfather of Soul, James Brown: Say it aloud—and loud!

9

Step Four—Writing It Down and Saying It Aloud

"The discipline of writing something down is the first step toward making it happen."—LEE IACOCCA

Here's the stark reality: If you don't write your goals down, you greatly limit your chances of completing them. Statistics reveal that only 3 percent of people set goals and only 1 percent of those who create them write them down. Contrast this with the fact that people who write their goals down increase their success rate by 42 percent.

Clearly, writing down your goals is a critical part of the process. More importantly, however, you must ensure that they are memorialized as a constant reminder of *what* you must get done; *why* you chose these goals; and the dates by *when* they must be accomplished. By taking this initiative, you help conquer the abstract, uncertain feeling that goals sometimes inflict upon the human brain, especially when problematic circumstances arise and limit forward progression.

Memorialize and Maintain

Some people—at work and/or in their personal lives—create goals on their computers in a Word or Excel document and then don't look at them again until a year later (if at all). Others might scribble them down as notes on a pad and rarely revisit them. Others may print out the goals and focus on them for a couple of weeks, but then lose steam when they don't see or feel immediate results. The incomplete goals begin to accumulate, fester, and nag at you until guilt and hopelessness kick in and then, finally, stagnation—as if they never existed in the first place.

My suggestion is that you make a conscious effort at least twice each day (i.e., morning and night) to review the goals, read them aloud to yourself (in a mirror, if that is impactful for you), and visualize them in your mind. As you do so, you are only thinking about one thing: successfully completing your goals. At this moment, you aren't problem-solving any obstacles, fretting about the due dates, or listening to the voices of naysayers in your head. You are reading aloud, visualizing, accepting, and *believing*.

This mindset shift doesn't require a one-size-fits-all process. It's about personal preference and style. Everyone has a different way of thinking and feeling; what works for one person may not be effective for another. In this chapter, I've laid out several options for you to consider. No matter what you choose, the general process is the same: say your goals aloud, picture them in your head, accept them, and then believe in them as if they are real. As you memorialize your goals, consider both the written words and their meaning as they filter through your mind, body, and soul. Otherwise, they risk becoming empty words on whatever medium you have chosen.

Lather, Wash, Rinse, Repeat

Boxing legend Mohammad Ali once said, "It's the repetition of affirmations that leads to belief. And once that belief becomes a deep conviction, things begin to happen." Norman Vincent Peale, author of the classic *The Power of Positive Thinking*, had a similar philosophy: "Repetition of the same thought or physical action develops into a habit, which repeated frequently enough, becomes an automatic reflex."

Your goals must become an intrinsic part of your daily life. This goes for much-needed days off as well, because you don't want to lose any of the work you've done to that point to build an automatic reflex. Think of this in terms of what a fitness trainer might say to you if you don't feel at your best that day to push yourself: "It's perfectly okay, don't sweat it. For today, all you want to do is *maintain* your routine and physical ability. You'll be able to increase your speed next time."

Perhaps the most powerful example of this for me occurred the year I retired from both the Navy Reserve and as a corporate engineer. I created and repeatedly declared the following two goal affirmations:

FIRST THING EVERY MORNING
I'm going to retire on December 31 of this year.

LAST THING EVERY NIGHT BEFORE BED
I'm going to retire on December 31 of this year.

As you can see, I was 100 percent committed to accomplishing my goal of retiring at the end of that year. According to my mentor, however, the morning and evening recitations weren't enough, and he convinced me to repeatedly write them down in my planner.

I sensed that he rightly detected a note of skepticism from me about this practice. I recall thinking at the time, "What's the big deal about writing something down? Isn't it stupid and redundant to write the same thing over and over?"

I eventually came to realize this isn't something magical like a Christmas gift wish that a child writes down and mails to Santa Claus in the North Pole. My mentor's advice was reinforced by myriad authorities at several conferences I attended. At one of these events, a couple of billionaires stressed the enormous value of writing things down—whether it concerns your goals or something else of importance—as it makes the concept tangible for you and, therefore, more likely to occur.

While attending a separate professional development/ networking event, I listened to a speaker discuss the fourth dimension and its relation to writing. I gleaned from his talk that, when you write something down, it takes something from the intangible fourth dimension and brings it into the second dimension of reality where we can now experience it. The concept resonated with me, and I have done it ever since.

Solving the Debate: Handwriting vs. Typing Your Goals

A great deal of research supports the theory that the act of writing things down by hand solidifies an idea in your mind infinitely more than from just typing on a keyboard or phone, enabling you to form a stronger commitment to it. The physical action of holding a writing implement is intimate and feels real and, therefore, seems more achievable. Note-taking by hand—as opposed to typing on a laptop or computer—can lead to "improved retention of content," according to a white paper by Michael C. Friedman at the Harvard Initiative for Learning and Teaching at Harvard University.

My goal to retire began as something floating around in my head. It didn't have much significance until I wrote it down with a date attached, at which point it became something completely different. Suddenly, it signaled *action*. If I hadn't written it down, I would have continued to kick this goal down the road. We all know how the mind works; procrastination sets in. You think to yourself, "I'll do it at some point, when the timing is right, and everything is in order, blah, blah, blah…"

Where to Write Them Down

Your choice of where you write down your goals and store them not only says a great deal about you but is also a determinant of your future success. Goals are a declaration of intent, which means their designated location demonstrates the extent of your commitment. There is a big difference between a goal handwritten in your prized leather journal that is almost always within reach vs. a typed statement in a Word document on your computer that you rarely, if ever, open.

In our digital world, mobile phones and digital watches can be useful, even fun tools. Some people store their goals on these devices, perhaps using an app, Calendar, or Notes. There is nothing wrong with using technology to help us achieve our objectives, but often they become distractions from focusing on the goals themselves. My view is there is nothing inherently special or meaningful about transcribing or reading a goal on a device. The most effective purpose of these tools is to help provide us with *reminders to review the goals* or complete some immediate action relevant to them.

A printed planner—when used properly—can be just as good as any journal. There are many options available, ranging from paper to flexible plastic to leather; it's all a matter of your personal preference, style, and budget. What makes the planner distinct from a generic calendar is that, like a journal, it can also serve as a place to commit to goals through the physical act of handwriting. Better yet, it can track times and dates and be available for use without having to plug anything in.

As I'm sure you've deduced by now, I use my planner for much more than just scheduling and planning. It serves as my primary source for writing down, reviewing, and reciting my goals at least twice a day. I carry it with me wherever I go and refer to it throughout the day to jot down ideas whenever an idea might hit me. It rests on my night table while I'm sleeping, so it's always available if something comes to me in the middle of the night.

I've discovered from many people—especially professional writers—that you can't rely on your memory to remember an idea. Things inevitably occur throughout the day that distract you and bury whatever brilliant concept came to you. Often, the idea vanishes from your mind forever.

If the idea is so important—or even if you are uncertain at that moment—write it in your planner or journal right away as is, before you forget it. Writing things down by hand improves your ability to commit the idea to memory, which means it will penetrate your subconscious and perhaps be improved upon without your even being aware of it.

Sure, if you are in a pinch, you can write things down on a napkin, envelope, legal pad, or in your Notes folder, but none of these objects looks or feels *special*. A planner or journal is imbued with the kind of formality and lasting importance that will help your goals retain their sacred luster.

In addition to a journal or planner, you can supplement goal storage wherever you think will be most beneficial to you in terms of keeping them front and center in your mind. This is where listing them at the top of your whiteboard in bright colors, taping them to your monitor or laptop, or placing Post-its on your refrigerator can provide subliminal reinforcement of their messaging throughout your day. There is no right or wrong here; do whatever works best to motivate you!

Symbolic Reminders

In Notre Dame Stadium, Indiana—home of the Notre Dame Fighting Irish football team—a three-foot, four-inch wooden sign painted gold with blue hand lettering hangs above the staircase in the tunnel that leads from the home team's locker room to the gridiron. The placard, which reads "Play Like a Champion Today," is positioned at just the right spot so that players trotting through the tunnel can reach up and touch it prior to heading onto the field.

I've always admired the inspirational impact this gesture has on Notre Dame players. Though they didn't create the phrase or personally handwrite the sign, the physical and symbolic act of touching it each time they pass by reminds them of their commitment to a shared goal.

Along these same lines, Michael Jordan's honored his commitment to his alma mater, the University of North Carolina, by wearing his old Carolina blue uniform shorts underneath his Chicago Bulls official uniform when he entered the NBA. The shorts were a physical reminder of his commitment to UNC, his roots, and why he chooses to compete on the court.

Goal Tending

In the TV series *Ted Lasso*, the titular character handwrites the word "BELIEVE" on a piece of paper and tapes it above his door. The personalized, informal message has the desired effect on the team, until it is ripped off the wall and cut apart. At this stage, Coach Lasso imbues the sign with yet another powerful message that prevents his players from losing faith: The act of *believing* comes from within, not from any exterior source.

As we look around, representations of our commitments and belief systems surround us all the time. What's a wedding ring, if not a tangible commitment to marriage? A cross, a Star of David, or other religious image emblazoned as jewelry around one's neck may serve as a symbolic reminder of one's faith. Taking this a step further, many people have tattoos etched directly on their skin to proclaim that their messages are so important they made them part of their being.

Of course, I'm not suggesting that you literally tattoo your goal on your arm (or any other area of your body). My point is that turning your goal into a ritual—such as by writing the goal down twice a day and repeating it aloud—results in placing it at the top of your mind. Consider it like medicine that you take in the morning that remains with you all day and through the night. By the following morning, the medicine has been absorbed and passed through your system, which means it's time for another dose. Ask yourself this question: *What ritual or symbolism can magnify my goal and make it as meaningful and memorable as possible?*

Consistency Is Key

Bill Belichick, the winningest head coach in National Football League history with six Super Bowl victories with the New England Patriots, once said, "It's not about the talent. It's about dependability, consistency, and being ability to improve."

I consulted with many professional writers as I researched this book. In doing so, I learned a great deal about their habits. Many of them readily admit that the act of writing is a constant struggle, which made me wonder: *How are they able to complete their manuscripts once they start, whereas so many others give up?*

The most frequent response I received was *consistency*. Almost every writer stated that they write almost every day (if not *every* day). They do this because the consistent ritual creates a rhythm that feeds itself throughout the day and even overnight until the writing picks up again the following morning.

By immersing themselves in their work, they are committing to it on a regular basis. Although this comparison specifically refers to actual writing (creating) and not just the process of writing down a goal, the repeated effort and practice yields the same positive results.

Remember the Hemingway quote in the last chapter regarding writing at least "one true sentence" every day? Writing down your goals at least twice a day, every day has the same effect on your psyche as writing hundreds of sentences. The repetition works its way into your habits, remains in your thoughts, generates momentum, and counts as a solid step in furthering progress toward completing your goals.

In this chapter, I provided all the tools you need to properly document and memorialize your goals. Unfortunately, despite our best intentions and efforts, we aren't necessarily equipped to always hold ourselves fully accountable. Sometimes we lose enthusiasm for our goals and gradually drift away from them. Other times, we become distracted or lazy. The worst is when we become so impatient with our goals that we take shortcuts, hindering our own potential. For these reasons, I saved this step for last: finding a suitable accountability partner.

10

Step Five—Finding a Suitable Accountability Partner

"He who walks with the wise grows wise, but a companion of fools suffers harm."—PROVERBS 13:20

In Chapter Three, I stated that one of the reasons S.M.A.R.T. goals are so effective is that they hold you accountable for completing them. Unfortunately, the first two mindset shifts—*abundance* and *believing is seeing*—sometimes aren't enough to keep the brain focused and powerful enough to conquer internal and external negativity, pressure, conflict, adversity, and roadblocks over the long term, as the passion, commitment, and memory necessary to support the goals begin to erode. This is when recruiting an accountability partner can become an invaluable asset for you. It's perfectly okay to admit that you can't always "go it alone," which means welcoming the support of someone else.

An accountability partner is a trusted person who provides encouragement, support, and advice when requested and as mutually agreed upon. This individual reminds you of the importance of sticking to your goals, helps you stay on course, and sometimes advises you what on you should and shouldn't do. A good accountability partner must be strong and provide tough love to you without casting any judgment. Cynicism and sarcasm are also verboten. Your accountability partner should be an advocate and ally who helps you stay on the path toward achieving your goals.

An Accountability Partner Isn't the Same as a Mentor

You want both a mentor and an accountability partner. The similarities in approach between the two are (1) commitment and (2) nonjudgmental support. However, while a mentor may hold you accountable at certain points, their main role is providing wise counsel (as explained in Step Two, Chapter Seven). A mentor aids the mentee by sharing their experiences, advising, empathizing, and sometimes offering recommendations and connections. Your mentor may even be part of your goal-setting process. The relationship often involves an understated hierarchy: a leader/follower paradigm. The mentor has the years of accomplishment behind them and knows more than you do; sometimes, you even pay for the counsel's valuable time.

By contrast, an accountability partner is there only to help you stay on track. They aren't providing lessons or direction—just reminders and encouragement.

To further distinguish the role of accountability partner, let's use a simple comparison: an exercise coach. This relationship can be one-sided (i.e., a trainer and trainee) or two-sided (i.e., a pair of friends who work out together). In the former, the trainer—usually, a paid provider—is holding their client accountable for showing up, learning the exercises, and putting in the hard work necessary to achieve mutually agreed upon goals. The trainer will provide encouragement and support while sometimes pushing the client but also sternly restating the goals when things seem to be flagging or heading in the wrong direction.

When it comes to *two-sided accountability*—what this step is all about—the relationship is mutual without either party having higher "rank" than the other. A good example would be two buddies (such as workout partners) who make a pact to hold each other accountable to meet their fitness goals. If one person skips a couple of training sessions or appears to be goofing around instead of doing the agreed-upon reps, the other is there to say, "Hey, come on, stick to the program. If *I'm* doing it, *you* have to do it. We made a deal, remember?"

Why do the above scenarios—one- and two-sided—work so well? I've heard from many people that, if they were responsible for exercising on their own, they would become lazy and the workout routines scattershot. Their goals wouldn't be met. However, with an accountability partner, they show up because they don't want to insult the other party. In general, people tend to be more respectful of other people's time more than their own.

Another upside of an accountability partner is that they can cajole you into performing at a higher level in real time rather than waiting for a scheduled session with your mentor. During a workout session, it's all too easy to get away with the "bare minimum." No one would ever know when you are just "phoning it in." But a trusted accountability partner can discern if you are coasting along and then give you a much-needed (but friendly) kick in the rump.

An Accountability Partner Proudly Stands Beside You

Accountability is a huge part of Naval culture. Although accountability partners aren't officially assigned, everyone functions and interacts as if such an unstated arrangement already exists. This isn't required; it's just part of the culture and something that is instilled in boot camp where everyone is broken down and built back up as a team. We are only as strong as the weakest link, trained to hold each other accountable to the rules. Whether you're a new recruit or a sailor transferred to another ship, the other crew members are there for you and have your back. Sailors who have been on a ship for a while recognize and understand the potential pitfalls newcomers inevitably face. They look out for you, ensuring you know the ropes and are adapting well.

The military offers a wide range of support for fresh recruits or those who are restationed in new roles. Every person's needs are a bit different, so you could tailor your accountability partner relationship (or mix and match), according to any of these tried-and-true arrangements:

- *Sea Daddys* ("Sea Mommas" for women): These experienced crew members provide a safety net and moral support, serving more as mentors than as accountability partners.

- *Liberty Buddies:* When sailors go on liberty (leave), these individuals ensure they stay safe and return to the ship on time.

- *Battle Buddies:* In combat or high-stress situations, sailors are paired to watch each other's backs and ensure mutual safety.

- *Fitness Partners:* Sailors often pair up to meet physical readiness standards, helping each other stay motivated and reach fitness goals.

- *Watch Team:* Sailors on watch duty are paired to ensure vigilance and adherence to protocols during their shifts.

- *Damage Control Teams:* During drills or actual emergencies, sailors work in pairs or teams to handle damage control, ensuring safety procedures are followed.

- *Maintenance Crews:* Sailors working on equipment or systems maintenance often work in pairs to verify work and ensure all procedures are correctly followed.

Finding the Right Accountability Partner

Of course, your accountability partner doesn't need to be a

sadistic drill instructor. Nor do they need to be the smartest person you know. It may take a while to identify the right person, so be patient. You want to identify someone who...

- Can be trusted with personal information

- Understands the general parameters of your field and your goals

- Knows you well enough to identify your quirks and where you might come up short

- Maintains a positive mindset

- Has accomplished many of their goals over the years

- Communicates directly and effectively

- Keeps their things in order

- Shows up on time

- Offers constructive criticism when needed without hesitation

- Provides encouragement and support

These are the things *to avoid* in an accountability partner:

- Self-absorption

- Unreliability or unavailability

- A "what could go wrong?" mentality

- A judgmental personality

- A harsh tone of voice

- Talks too much and doesn't listen

In the case of a two-sided accountability partnership, this should be reciprocal: You need to be the one who fulfills the above criteria for the other person as well. In other words, you want to walk the walk and talk the talk. This means checking yourself to avoid negativity and a harsh tone. You need to know when to speak versus listen and be supportive versus dole out tough love. You must be available as needed and fully present when you are the one being consulted. The partnership will only work if both parties put in the same amount of time and energy, have skin in the game, and call each other out when they detect a self-limiting belief.

How I Found the Right Accountability Partner

As my business started getting more serious, I found myself struggling to garner enough courage and strength to raise capital. I feared this part of the business, especially when I had to make presentations to wealthy prospects. I procrastinated and set up my own roadblocks, which only delayed progress on my goals and made me feel a bit cowardly.

I recognized that I desperately needed an accountability partner, but my mind resisted the notion. I thought to myself, "Why would I want to bring in someone who would force me into doing something I dislike and makes me afraid?"

Deep down, though, I knew I needed support and had to find someone—the *right* person. I was never going to achieve my goals if I couldn't get past this hurdle. While I had a mentor who was perfect for me in many respects, he was at a much higher rung on the ladder than me and, therefore, an inappropriate accountability partner. It would have been like asking the head chef at a Michelin Star restaurant to wait on tables.

One evening, my mentor held a social gathering for professionals in the real estate space. During the festivities, I overheard a guy talking about his time in the Navy aboard a submarine. I assumed he was in the nuclear space, since more people assigned to a submarine are nuclear trained (as I was) versus conventional trained (aka non-nuclear). The nuclear Navy is a small niche within the Navy, so there was a good chance we would have much in common.

I approached him as we stood on the food line. We connected right away. During our conversation, I confirmed that, not only was he in the nuclear power field but he was also an engineer. As if that wasn't enough of a coincidence, he subsequently worked in the private sector and then entered real estate. The differences between us were in terms of success and experience. He was about six years ahead of me and already doing what I wanted to do.

He was a bit ahead of me, but he checked off all the other boxes, so I asked him if he would be willing to serve as my accountability partner and vice versa. Although it wasn't a 100 percent even two-sided arrangement—since he had more to offer to me than I did for him—there were still areas where I could add value to him. He agreed without hesitation.

Goal Tending

You may also want to form a team of people I refer to as the *inner circle*. Essentially, they become your support group, your cheerleaders.

Look around in your personal and professional life and jot down all the people you know and can rely upon who are nonjudgmental and provide unconditional support. (Your accountability partner may be included in this group, but not your mentor.) Among the names you listed, which five rise to the top in terms of proximity to power (see Chapter Five) and know more than you do about your business area? Which ones would you trust by your side in a foxhole if you were surrounded by enemy fire?

This inner circle might be the people on your bowling team, your fishing trip companions, your fellow religious congregation members, your fraternity/sorority pals, your book club members, or your football watching buddies. They keys are *trust*, *encouragement*, and *positivity*. For example, if your presentation bombed and you failed to raise necessary capital, you want these five or so people to listen, be sympathetic, and say things such as: "We're here for you," "Everyone experiences setbacks, don't sweat it," and "We believe in you."

We set up a plan in which we would talk three or four times a week at night, after our kids were in bed. During these sessions, we would ask each other direct questions about what we had or hadn't done since our last conversation. *How did your presentation go? Did you make all your offers? Did you follow up? Did you attend that networking event?*

We also discussed our specific markets and matters pertaining to our individual companies. While we were both in real estate, we were reaching different markets and, therefore, non-competitive with each other. Not only that but our outside perspectives also helped in ways we couldn't have foreseen.

I never wanted to disappoint my accountability partner, and I believe he felt the same. During the day, there was always a part of me that heard his voice in my head, urging me to do what I agreed upon. There was also a piece of my mind that opened for him, so I could offer things that might benefit him. As a result of this mutually beneficial relationship, I never again faltered to accomplish my goals due to fear.

Note that it is possible to sometimes "outgrow" an accountability partner, which has happened to me a few times over the years. You might feel that, while they helped guide you to reach your current level, the person doesn't have the requisite knowledge to take you any further. This isn't a knock against this valuable person but rather, a sign that the relationship has come to its natural end. It's okay at this stage to be honest and explain your decision to move on in a professional and sensitive way. You can remain friends, of course, but you don't want to become stagnant or have stale sessions with someone just for the sake of it. A new accountability partner every few years helps add fresh perspective and further your growth along your journey.

Congratulations! Now that you have gone through my five steps, you are well on your way to overcoming your own road-blocks and accomplishing your goals—and so much more. I just have one thing to share—a bonus, if you will.

11

A Special Bonus—Zones

"The comfort zone is a beautiful place, but nothing ever grows there."—JOHN ASSARAF

check-source?

When you boil it all down, goal setting is about one thing: producing results. To achieve those results, I've devised a daily system inspired by my Navy experience that further ensures that your goal-related tasks get done every single day: *zones*.

Almost everything in the Navy, especially performance, is measured as a stoplight chard of red, yellow, and green. An admiral typically has several slides of stoplight charts that help them review the status of each area of the fleet. The commanders of those vessels have additional stoplight charts to monitor the health of all weapons systems, progress of personnel and training, condition of equipment, and so forth.

There are three types of zones, each of which is associated with a color: Green (good), Yellow (middle), and Red (bad). You want to focus most of your time on activities that fall into the Green Zone. This is where your effort results in direct, measurable benefits, such as closing a deal or generating revenue.

The Yellow Zone includes activities that are peripheral to the goal and somewhat productive. Good examples of this would be polishing your sales presentation or conducting background research on the company you are about to pitch. Activities in this zone would not directly generate revenue but may provide indirect support or improve a future situation.

As for the Red Zone—it's kind of self-explanatory. This is when the activity (such as watching YouTube cat videos) doesn't do anything to further your goals. In fact, it could be a waste of time and counterproductive. While we are all entitled to have our breaks and enjoy life, our priority should be toward accomplishing our goals. If we spend too much time in the Red Zone, our goals simply won't get done.

The rule of thumb is that 75 percent of your time when you're in growth mode must be spent on Green Zone activities, 20 percent on Yellow Zone tasks that support the Green Zone, and 5 percent at most on Red Zone. In an eight-hour workday, for example, this translates to six hours in the Green, an hour and a half in the Yellow, and a half hour in the Red. (Of course, many driven entrepreneurs and ambitious professionals put in more than eight hours per day, so these percentages could apply to *all* waking hours.) By setting limits on how much time you spend in each zone, you increase focus on your goal-related tasks and avoid procrastination and distractions.

Tim Ferriss, author of *The Four-Hour Workweek*, said it best: "Focus on being productive instead of busy."

Now, go be productive!

Keep It Going!

*Congratulations! You have now completed the five steps of my pro-*gram with my bonus and are well armed to head out into the world with your powerful goals. If you follow my instructions and tips, you will not only maintain your goals but far exceed them.

I can't emphasize enough that no matter how successful you become, some people are always going to tell you what they think what you should or shouldn't do, often with the best of intentions. This might include parents, close relatives, friends, teachers, professors, supervisors, colleagues, coaches, recruiters, HR departments, or extended family. I would even add one more to this list: your social media community, on which everyone—sometimes total strangers in your network—has an opinion and will express it in the bluntest terms, whether they understand the situation or not.

Remember: You are in control of your destiny. If you have a unique vision for the next phase of your life or career and enough passion to sustain it, *go for it*—even if it means heading on a completely new path from your prior direction and might involve some measure of risk. You have only one life to live and a limited number of hours on this planet, so I advise spending your time well and taking that calculated chance.

Your next step? To paraphrase Dr. Greg S. Reid, whose words grace the epilogue page of this book: Write your dream down with the date. Turn it into a goal, following my five steps. Break it down further and it will become a plan. Then back the plan with action, as this will make your dreams come true.

While I expect you to hunker down and stay focused, I hope you will also balance your life with fun things to do in the company of supportive people who make you feel good. It's vitally important to eat well, exercise, and do whatever else you can to relax, reduce stress, and maintain your sanity. There isn't a goal on earth that will ever be worth sacrificing your mental, emotional, or physical health—or the happiness of you and your loved ones.

Without further distraction… *put this book down* and *get to work*!

Sources

Part One

Chapter One

Aristotle: "Knowing yourself is the beginning of all wisdom."
https://www.goodreads.com/quotes/3102-knowing-yourself-is-the-
 beginning-of-all-wisdom

Douglas Vermeeren, "Why People Fail to Achieve Their Goals,"
 ReliablePlant.com. https://www.reliableplant.com/Read/8259/fail-
 achieve-goals

Jim Clifton, "The World's Broken Workplace," Gallup, June 13, 2017.
 https://news.gallup.com/opinion/chairman/212045/world-
 broken-workplace.aspx?g_source=position1&g_medium=related&g_
 campaign=tiles

Chapter Two

Buddha: "All that we are is the result of what we have thought."
https://www.thezengateway.com/culture/the-dhammapada-intro-
 duced-and-translated-by-eknath-easwaran

LinkedIn's vision: 'To create economic opportunity for every member
 of the global workforce.'"
https://economicgraph.linkedin.com/about

Apple's mission statement: "To bring the best user experience to customers through innovative hardware, software, and services."
https://businessmodelanalyst.com/apple-mission-and-vision-
 statement/

Dick's Sporting Goods purpose statement: "We create confidence
and excitement by personally equipping all athletes to achieve their
dreams.'"
"Best Purpose Statement Examples from the Fortune 500,"
PurposeBrand.com, August 16, 2021.
https://purposebrand.com/blog/best-purpose-statements-fortune-500/

"Business Values," Business Queensland.
https://www.business.qld.gov.au/running-business/planning/
values#types-of-business-values

Chief of Naval Operations Navigation Plan 2022. https://media.defense.
gov/2022/Jul/26/2003042389/-1/-1/1/NAVIGATION
%20PLAN%202022_SIGNED.PDF

Megan Eckstein, "Navy Moves to Align Its Strategy with
National Defense Strategy Priorities," DefenseNews,com, July 26,
2022.
https://www.defensenews.com/naval/2022/07/26/navy-moves-
to-align-its-strategy-with-national-defense-strategy-priorities/

Oliver Maximovich, "7 Business Strategy Examples." Plerdy.com,
February 4, 2024.
https://www.plerdy.com/blog/business-strategy-examples/#:~:
text=Let%27s%20take%20the%20example%20of,coffee%20
between%20home%20and%20work.

Chapter Three

Zig Ziglar: "A goal properly set is halfway reached."
https://www.brainyquote.com/quotes/zig_ziglar_380875

G. T. Doran, G. T., "There's a S.M.A.R.T. Way to Write Management's
Goals and Objectives," *Management Review* 70, no. 11: 35–36.

Part Two

Chapter Four

Norman Vincent Peale: "Change your thoughts and you change your world." https://www.brainyquote.com/quotes/norman_vincent_peale_130593

Dr. Lou E. Whitaker, "How Does Thinking Positive Thoughts Affect Neuroplasticity?" *Meteor Education.*
https://meteoreducation.com/how-does-thinking-positive-thoughts-affect-neuroplasticity/#:~:text=What%20is%20going%20on%20in,a%20feeling%20of%20well%2Dbeing.

"How Our Thoughts Affect Our Mental Health," MindHealth360.
https://www.mindhealth360.com/contributor/negative-thought-patterns-and-beliefs/#:~:text=Repeated%20negative%20thoughts%2C%20such%20as,Insomnia

"Try Recognizing Other Patterns of Automatic Negative Thinking," Healthline.
https://www.healthline.com/health/mental-health/stop-automatic-negative-thoughts#2-recognize-automatic-negative-thinking

"Rocky Is Afraid" (Rocky III).
https://www.youtube.com/watch?v=BXPgmSm0xDc

Melissa Sartore, "16 Historical Underdogs Who Came Out on Top," Ranker.com, February 28, 2022.
https://www.ranker.com/list/underdogs-in-history-who-won/melissa-sartore

Evan Andrews, "7 Amazing Rags to Riches Stories." History.com, August 29, 2018.
https://www.history.com/news/7-amazing-rags-to-riches-stories

ABC News, "Erin Brockovich: The Real Story of the Town Three Decades Later," June 10, 2021.
https://abcnews.go.com/US/erin-brockovich-real-story-town-decades/story?id=78180219

Chapter Five

Steve Maraboli: "Once your mindset changes, everything on the outside will change along with it."
https://quotefancy.com/quote/50051/Steve-Maraboli-Once-your-mindset-changes-everything-on-the-outside-will-change-along-with

Psylent Dart, "The Mindset of a Champion in Sport." Medium.com, July 18, 2020.
https://medium.com/@akarshagru/mindset-psychology-of-success-part-3-bb60eb1d4edf

DiamondMind Online, "The Life and Career of Revolutionary Baseball GM Billy Beane."
https://imaginesports.com/news/revolutionary-baseball-gm-billy-beane

Neale Donald Walsch, *Conversations with God*, 1996.

J.D. Meier, "Stephen Covey on Integrity, Maturity, and an Abundance Mentality." SourcesofInsight.com.
https://sourcesofinsight.com/integrity-maturity-and-abundance/

Steven R. Covey, *The 7 Habits of Highly Effective People: 30th Anniversary Edition*. Simon & Schuster, 2020.

"10 Stars Who Were Rejected Before Making It Big." Heart.com.
https://www.heart.co.uk/showbiz/10-stars-who-were-rejected-before-making-it-big/steven-spielberg/

Jordan Ruimy, "Alfred Hitchcock Did Not Like Steven Spielberg and Refused to Meet Him: Isn't That the Boy Who Made That Fish Movie?" WorldofReel.com, December 30, 2022.
https://www.worldofreel.com/blog/2022/12/fnbej7t78z07p2ra87in-vt74p9lklg#:~:text=The%20legendary%20director%20of%20%E2%80%9DVertigo,repeatedly%20refused%20to%20meet%20Spielberg.

Anthony Breznican, "The Odd David Lynchian Story Behind David Lynch's Cameo in *The Fabelmans*," *Vanity Fair,* February 14, 2023.
https://www.vanityfair.com/hollywood/2023/02/david-lynch-spielberg-fabelmans

Aimee Groth, "You're the Average of the Five People You Spend the Most Time With," *Business Insider.*
https://www.businessinsider.com/jim-rohn-youre-the-average-of-the-five-people-you-spend-the-most-time-with-2012-7

Part Three

Chapter Six

Franklin D. Roosevelt: "The only limit to our realization of tomorrow will be our doubts of today."
https://www.loc.gov/resource/rbpe.24204300/?st=text

Napoleon Hill, *Think and Grow Rich.* TarcherPerigee, 2007.

Ian Kenney, "The Visualization Secret: What Successful Business Leaders Have in Common." LinkedIn, April 8, 2023.
https://www.linkedin.com/pulse/visualization-secret-what-successful-business-leaders-i-kenney

Jessica Rovello, "Five Ways Katie Ludecky, Michael Phelps, and Other Olympians Visualize Success." *Inc.,* August 23, 2016.
https://www.inc.com/jessica-rovello/five-steps-to-visualize-success-like-an-olympian.html

Brian Cain, "Evan Longoria: E60 The Best Mental Game of Baseball."
https://www.youtube.com/watch?v=y3vkUm54adI

Katherine Hurst. "Celebrities and the Law of Attraction Success Stories," April 23, 2018.
https://thelawofattraction.com/celebrities-law-attraction/

Peter Achinstein, "Evidence for Molecules: Jean Perrin and Molecular Reality," in *The Book of Evidence, Oxford Academic,* 2001.
https://academic.oup.com/book/5529/chapter-abstract/148483192?redirectedFrom=fulltext

Bianca Weiland, "The Science Behind Visualization." Activacuity.com, January 24, 2016.
https://www.activacuity.com/2016/01/the-science-behind-visualization/

Dr. Joe Dispenza, "The Power of Thoughts." https://www.youtube.com/watch?v=XWbVL1YmUxo

Dr. Joe Dispenza, "Everything You Visualize Will Come True!" https://www.youtube.com/watch?v=qazR30DIsOM

Dr. Joe Dispenza, "Observing a Research Milestone: Meditation's Impact and Influence on Immunity," August 15, 2023.
https://drjoedispenza.com/dr-joes-blog/observing-a-research-milestone-meditations-impact-and-influence-on-immunity

"The Power of Visualization."
https://www.facebook.com/watch/?v=595099294825254

Rachel Lit, "What Happens When You Meditate," *Stanford Magazine,* March 13, 2023.
https://stanfordmag.org/contents/what-happens-when-you-meditate#:~:text=Levels%20of%20dopamine%20(the%20neurotransmitter,they%20send%20signals%20more%20routinely.

"Michael Phelps Biography," Olympic.com.
https://olympics.com/en/athletes/michael-phelps-ii

Nathan Sellers. "Michael Phelps Won When Things Went Wrong! How? Visualize Yourself to Success."
https://www.youtube.com/watch?v=1BAzOlXpRSc

Chapter Seven

Warren Buffett: "Tell me who your heroes are, and I'll tell you who you'll turn out to be."
https://www.azquotes.com/quote/882451#google_vignette

Chapter Eight

Stephen Covey: "Begin with the end in mind."
https://www.franklincovey.com/the-7-habits/habit-2/

"Working Backwards (The Amazon Method)," AirFocus.com.
https://airfocus.com/glossary/what-is-working-backwards/#:
~:text=The%20%E2%80%9Cworking%20backwards%E2
%80%9D%20method%2C,by%20product%20teams%20at%20
Amazon.

Edgar Allan Poe, "The Philosophy of Composition." PoetryFoundation.
com, undated (original 1846).
https://www.poetryfoundation.org/articles/69390/the-
philosophy-of-composition

"All you have to do is write one true sentence. Write the truest sentence
that you know."
"Ernest M. Hemingway." PoetryFoundation.com.
https://www.poetryfoundation.org/poets/ernest-m-hemingway

Chapter Nine

Lee Iacocca: "The discipline of writing something down is the first step
toward making it happen."
https://www.brainyquote.com/quotes/lee_iacocca_149249

Banu Akgul, "The Power of Writing Down Goals: 42% More Likely to
Achieve Success." LinkedIn, March 16, 2023.
https://www.linkedin.com/pulse/power-writing-down-goals-42-more-
likely-achieve-success-banu-akgul/

Michael C. Friedman, "Notes on Note-Taking: Review of Research and
Insights for Students and Instructors," Harvard.com.
https://hwpi.harvard.edu/files/hilt/files/notetaking_0.pdf

Chapter Ten

Proverbs 13:20: "He who walks with the wise grows wise, but a companion of fools suffers harm."
https://www.biblegateway.com/verse/en/Proverbs%2013%3A20

Chapter Eleven

Author Unknown: "The comfort zone is a beautiful place, but nothing ever grows there."
https://deepstash.com/idea/8417/a-comfort-zone-is-a-beautiful-place-but-nothing-ever

Justin Bryant, "Focus on Being Productive Instead of Busy—Tim Ferriss," SelfMadeSuccess.com, April 18, 2016.

About the Author

Gary MacDermid was born and raised in Silver Spring, Maryland, and enlisted in the United States Navy directly after graduating high school. Gary earned a bachelor's degree in electrical engineering and was accepted into the Navy's prestigious nuclear power program. As a commissioned Naval Officer, he navigated warships through some of the most dangerous passages in the world. After retiring from the Navy as a Lieutenant Commander, Gary worked as a licensed Professional Engineer, performing design and analysis for nuclear power plants across the country. Then, founding USA Private Equities, he made the transition from electrical engineer to cash flow engineer and realized his goal of professional independence as he manages an investment portfolio designed to provide home ownership opportunities to those in need. He is living his dreams as a keynote speaker, motivating people worldwide to set and achieve high-reaching goals. Gary resides in the Phoenix, Arizona area. For more information, visit his website: garymacdermid.com.